Cambridge English Readers

Level 6

Series editor: Philip Prowse

He Knows Too Much

Alan Maley

D1005465

CAMBRIDGE
UNIVERSITY PRESS

PUBLISHED BY THE PRESS SYNDICATE OF THE UNIVERSITY OF CAMBRIDGE
The Pitt Building, Trumpington Street, Cambridge, United Kingdom

CAMBRIDGE UNIVERSITY PRESS
The Edinburgh Building, Cambridge CB2 2RU, UK
40 West 20th Street, New York, NY 10011–4211, USA
477 Williamstown Road, Port Melbourne, VIC 3207, Australia
Ruiz de Alarcón 13, 28014 Madrid, Spain
Dock House, The Waterfront, Cape Town 8001, South Africa

http://www.cambridge.org

First published 1999
Eighth printing 2004

Printed in India by Thomson Press

Typeset in 12/15pt Adobe Garamond [CE]

ISBN 0 521 65607 9

Contents

Characters

Dick Sterling: general manager in Madras, India of Trakton, a multinational manufacturing company.

Sally Sterling: Dick's wife.

Keith Lennox: Dick's boss at Trakton. Works in Delhi.

Barbara Lennox: Keith's wife.

Visvanathan (Vish): office manager at Trakton.

Molly: Vish's wife. She also works at Trakton.

Ramanathan (Ramu): Dick's personal assistant at Trakton.

Nagarajan: in Accounts at Trakton.

Lakshmi: Nagarajan's daughter.

Ned Outram: a former employee at Trakton.

Sir Percy Hancock: former chief executive of Trakton, once head of the Delhi office.

Sir Jeremy Jackson (Jacko): retired professor of comparative philology at Cambridge.

John Verghese.

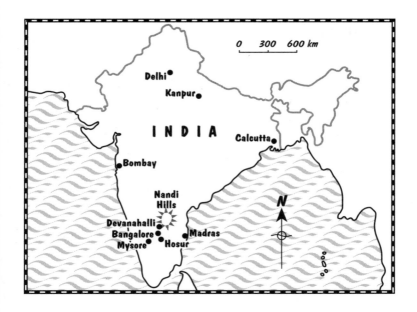

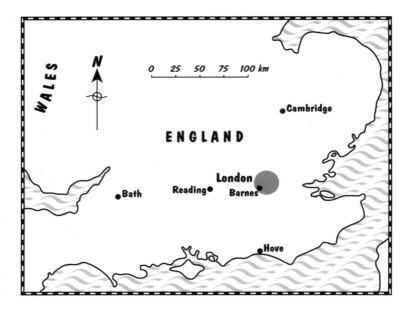

Chapter 1   *Madras 1986*

'He knows too much. I must ask you to do nothing.'

'But this time I caught him in the act. I have proof, witnesses, everything. There is no possible doubt. Surely . . .'

'I said he knows too much! The company can't afford to have any problems. Our position is very sensitive in this country. We can't afford to take risks. I am telling you once again – you will do nothing. And if there is any trouble, I'm afraid I shall have to hold you personally responsible. So be sensible for once in your life.'

'I see. So you are telling me to close my eyes to corruption and behave as if nothing has happened. Is that right?'

'I didn't put it quite like that. But, if you insist, yes. What Vish does or doesn't do is a minor matter compared with the company's global strategy. Just try to get things in perspective. After all, you won't be stuck in Madras for ever – I'll make sure that you're not. So just go with the flow for a bit longer. When you're in your next post this will all seem a very long way away, I can assure you. But meantime, no trouble. I hope I've made myself clear. Oh, and, by the way, I advise you to forget that we have had this conversation. Goodbye.'

Dick Sterling put the phone down. His hands were trembling. He was furious with himself for failing to persuade his boss in Delhi, Keith Lennox, to support him, and was disgusted at the mixture of veiled threats and vague promises Lennox had made. 'He knows too much' – the words still rang in his ears. He wondered, not for the last time, just what it was that Vish, the office manager of the factory, knew. How could it be so important that the company's position in India could be threatened by it? It simply didn't make sense.

Dick glanced at his watch. Four o'clock. He called for his driver, Gopal, and asked to be driven home. He'd had enough for the day. On his way out he passed Vish in the corridor. Vish was a small, fat man who waddled slightly when he walked. His ugly smile revealed two large teeth and his small eyes reminded Dick of a snake. Was it his imagination, or was the man smiling to himself? His snake eyes glinted with self satisfaction, almost as if he knew he was safe, protected.

Dick's car left the Trakton office and made its way slowly along the dusty, bumpy road leading south into the centre of Madras, towards his home. Even though Dick passed these buildings every day, they never lost their fascination for him. No one style dominated this city of contrasts where majestic but neglected colonial buildings stood next to modern glass and concrete banks, slum huts built from mud and roofed with coconut palms, ramshackle groups of shops selling everything from used car tyres to Indian-made foreign liquor[1] ... And where the traffic was a chaos of vehicles competing anarchically for the few overcrowded spaces on the roads. The journey home would take a long time.

Dick sat gloomily in the back of the car, going over in his mind the events which had led up to the present crisis.

How had he got himself into this impossible situation? It should never have happened, yet somehow, looking back, it seemed inevitable. Perhaps he was beginning to believe in fate?

He had arrived three years earlier to take over as general manager of Trakton's factory in Madras. Trakton had been in India since before Independence. It had started out manufacturing military vehicles during the war and switched to commercial vehicles and earth-moving equipment when the war ended. Because of its key importance in helping to build the country's industrial base, it had not been completely taken over following Independence.

Though the Indian operation was technically independent, Trakton's corporate headquarters in London still had overall control. India was, of course, only one of the many countries in which Trakton operated. Dick had been transferred to Madras from Nigeria in fact, after a series of other overseas appointments. Each of the overseas factories had a general manager appointed from headquarters to oversee the management of the local workforce. In India this had worked particularly well. The Indian staff was highly-trained and efficient. They were also generally easy to work with; the company's enlightened industrial relations policy had made sure of that. Salaries were higher than the average, there was a good pensions scheme and generous health insurance benefits. Trakton boasted that it had not lost a day in strikes for over fifteen years.

Dick had found his senior Indian colleagues particularly good to work with. They knew their jobs inside out and were clearly committed to the company. Many of them had been with Trakton for the whole of their working lives, starting in the factory and working their way up to become managers. They were a good team.

The only exceptions had been Visvanathan, or 'Vish' as he was known, the office manager, and his wife Molly. Molly was in charge of the Personnel Department. For reasons Dick had only gradually understood, Vish and Molly were regarded by the rest of the senior staff as somehow 'special'. They behaved as if they had special privileges and expected other staff to defer to them. Dick slowly realised that they controlled other staff members through a combination of threats and promises. Given their positions, they could make life very difficult for anyone who opposed them. Likewise, they could make life easy for those who did what they wanted.

Dick knew that this sort of behaviour happened to varying degrees in every culture and didn't think much of it. Indeed, in the first few weeks after his arrival, both Vish and Molly had been all smiles and helpfulness.

'You'll need a driving licence. Don't worry. I know someone in the police. We'll fix it for you. There's no need for you to worry about any of these things. Just let me know and I'll take care of it,' Vish had said.

They had invited Dick and his wife Sally to dinner too. Their newly-built house was in the fashionable, up-and-coming Kalakshetra Colony,[2] close to the sea. Dick had been suitably impressed by the expensively-furnished house, which was full of the most modern household equipment. He had half-wondered, innocently, whether Vish had had to borrow money to pay for it all. Molly was justifiably proud of her collection of Indian temple carvings, southern Indian bronze statues and contemporary paintings.

They had invited a selection of their 'closest friends': a High Court judge, a police inspector, an IAS[3] officer, an architect, an ex-Minister of Finance in the State Government, the owner of a shipping company, a couple from the British High Commission, a Tamil[4] film director and a well-known local painter. Dick felt slightly uneasily, that these people had been invited to prove to him how well-connected the Visvanathans were. It had been a pleasant evening nonetheless. It was only later that Dick recalled seeing two members of the office staff helping to serve the meal. He also noted that there had been no shortage of genuine Scotch whisky, a drink not easily available on the local market.

It was not long, however, before Dick began experiencing another side to the Visvanathans. One morning he had gone into Vish's office unexpectedly for an informal chat. He found his office manager stamping his feet with rage, screaming abuse at one of the junior drivers. Papers and files had been thrown on the floor. Dick asked Vish to follow him to his office. There he had suggested that perhaps less dramatic personnel management techniques should be used in future. Vish had not liked the criticism. His small snake-like eyes had almost disappeared in the fat folds of his face. He had continued to clench and unclench his hands throughout the brief interview. Sweat ran in streams down his neck. He had left the office soon after the interview and remained away on 'sick leave' for two more days.

Soon afterwards, Molly went to see Dick about the promotion of a senior driver to a supervisor's position in the Stores. She recommended the man's attitude and suitability for the job. Dick had therefore promoted the man. It was only several weeks later that Dick discovered that another equally well-qualified staff member had also applied for the promotion. 'Unfortunately' his papers had been 'mislaid' by the Personnel Department and had never reached Dick. When Dick had questioned her about it, Molly had raised her eyes to the ceiling and sighed.

'Now you can see what I have to put up with, Dick,' she cooed. 'They're all so unreliable. The papers were under a pile of files on Shivkumar's desk. I've told him so many times. I really think we should consider transferring him. What do you think?'

'I think you should deal with all applications in person from now on,' Dick had gently suggested.

'I suppose you're right. But my workload is already so heavy. And isn't it a good thing for us to train the juniors to take more responsibility?' She gazed at him quite shamelessly with her liquid black eyes. She had more charm than her husband and Dick could see that some people would think she was attractive. He realised, looking at her, that there was nothing much he could do, unless he wanted a major row.

Chapter 2   *Family life*

Dick was woken from his thoughts as the car screeched to a stop to avoid an auto-rickshaw[5] and a scooter carrying a family of four which had cut across the crowded road outside the High Court buildings. Dick's mind came back to the present. For anyone with strong nerves, travelling in India is a constant source of interest and surprise.

His driver Gopal inched his way forward, successfully winning a few feet from a bus cutting in on one side and a water-tanker on the other, each puffing out clouds of billowing, black diesel fumes. The road widened as they passed Fort St George. Gopal speeded up and they were soon leaving the elegant but neglected university buildings behind. They drove the length of the Marina, the sea on the left and a succession of historic buildings on the right. Even at this hour a few people were strolling along the beach taking the early evening air. Soon there would be crowds, all escaping the oven heat of the city for the cooling evening sea breeze.

It was five-thirty before they reached the tree-lined shade of Boat Club Road and the calm of Dick's company house, set well back from the road in its own garden. The chowkidar[6] opened the gate and the car slid gratefully into the cool shade of the porch.

There was a note on the kitchen table from Dick's wife, Sally, to say she was out to tea with one of the awful society women who seemed to form a permanent part of their social life. She reminded him that they were to attend a drinks party at the Jussawallahs, a Parsee[7] couple they had met at the club the previous week. He groaned, then made his way to the bathroom for a shower.

Later, as he sat drinking a cool beer on the terrace overlooking the garden, Dick's thoughts returned to his present problems. He was forty-eight years old; no longer young but still young enough to rise in the company. He was in good shape physically – six feet tall, slim and muscular, even if his hair was prematurely grey. He had worked for Trakton since leaving university. They had sent him to some pretty hard countries when he was young – Papua New Guinea, Ecuador, Iran, Saudi Arabia. He had always managed to do well, even in the most difficult conditions.

And he had paid the price; his first wife, Sarah, had died of malaria in Papua New Guinea. At twenty-four he had found himself a widower and father of a baby daughter, Angie. She was grown up now but he still recalled the desperation of those weeks and months following Sarah's death. For a time he had gone to pieces, drinking heavily and moving from one unsuitable woman to another.

It was only when he returned briefly to London, between jobs, that he met Sally. They had both been invited to a drinks party at the Ecuadorian Embassy. He was to leave for Quito a month later. She was working as a secretary at the Foreign Office. On the surface, they had nothing in common. She was from an upper-class family with a town house in Knightsbridge and a place in the country near Bath. She had no need to work, but her father, an ex-ambassador himself, had arranged for her to work at the Foreign Office, partly at least, in the hope that she would find 'someone suitable' to marry. Instead she fell hopelessly in love with Dick; a man without money, with a dubious reputation, and with a baby daughter to bring up into the bargain. It would have been difficult to find anyone less 'suitable'. But when they woke together the next morning in Dick's Bayswater[8] flat, it seemed the most natural thing in the world. Sally's family had disapproved of their relationship, but she left for Quito with Dick after a brief and quiet civil marriage in Kensington Registry Office. No-one from Sally's family had attended.

Their life together had been a great success, though not without its ups and downs. Sally had been a wonderful mother to Angie, and they had had Simon a year after their marriage. They still enjoyed each other's company, even if they were very much absorbed in their own concerns: Dick with Trakton, Sally with raising funds for a children's charity she was involved with. There were many days when they scarcely saw each other.

Dick thought about Vish again. He had long suspected that the man was dishonest but he had never been able to prove it before. Dick's suspicions centred on the way the company awarded contracts for various kinds of building and maintenance work. It seemed to Dick that the costs for this kind of work were higher than they should be. Contracts also seemed to be always awarded to the same few companies, many of them owned by personal friends of Vish. He suspected that Vish was taking a percentage from the contractors in exchange for giving them the contract. But for a long time Dick had never been able to prove this. When questioned, Vish had always had very clever reasons for selecting one contractor rather than another, cheaper, one.

It was only when the building contractor Haridas Enterprises came directly to Dick to complain they had not been awarded a contract for building Trakton's new factory at Hosur that Dick had found real evidence. Haridas Enterprises had complained that the twenty per cent they had formerly paid to Vish had been increased to twenty-five per cent. When they had refused to pay, Vish had given the contract to another company, Naveen Construction, who had obviously agreed to pay him the higher rate. Haridas had provided Dick with all the evidence he needed about previous contracts.

Dick understood that, in different cultures, people did different favours for each other. Sometimes it was called corruption, sometimes it wasn't. Dick wanted to be careful in judging Vish.

It was the contract for the factory in Hosur, which was really big money, that convinced Dick that Vish was really corrupt. It was for a project which was worth many crores[9] of rupees and would last at least three years. If Vish was getting twenty-five per cent of the total cost he was going to make a lot of money out of this. At last Dick had something really big to charge Vish with – and hard evidence too. So earlier that day he had called Vish and presented him with the evidence. It had been a stormy meeting! Vish had clearly never been challenged in this way before. He had sweated, he had shouted, he had protested his innocence, he had threatened ... It was after this meeting that Dick had phoned his boss, the director of Trakton, Keith Lennox.

His thoughts were interrupted by Sally's arrival.

'Hello, darling,' she said as she bent to kiss him on the cheek. 'How was your day?'

'Terrible. I don't want to talk about it now – I confronted Vish this morning and then had a row on the phone with Keith Lennox about it. I just can't understand Keith's attitude.'

'Don't you think you're getting a bit obsessed with the Visvanathans, darling?' said Sally. 'After all, you are the boss. Surely, if you have proof of whatever it is, all you have to do is sack them?'

'If only life was that simple!' sighed Dick with an air of tiredness. 'Who are we going to this evening?'

'Come on, don't pretend you've forgotten them. They're that nice couple we met at the club last week.' Sally seemed genuinely upset that he hadn't remembered. 'He owns a shipping company. You should be interested in that at least. Anyway, do try to stay awake this time!'

Dick went up to the bedroom half an hour later to find Sally coming out of the shower. He dried her with one of their biggest bath towels. They kissed and one thing led to another so that they arrived an hour late for the party, though no-one seemed to notice. The rest of the evening was spent in dull and empty conversations. They returned at midnight and Dick immediately fell into a dreamless sleep.

Chapter 3 *Threatening shadows: Delhi, January 1987*

In the following weeks, Dick began to receive anonymous, poison-pen letters. These were usually written using letters cut from the newspaper and stuck crudely onto a sheet of paper. They accused him of a variety of things, mainly of a sexual nature.

There were about a dozen such letters. At first Dick was amused, then angry, then worried. Of course he was innocent of the accusations but even a rumour could be damaging, both to him and to the company. He had asked Indian friends for advice. They told him to ignore the letters – the city was full of jealous madmen. Many of his friends too had received such letters in the past. They would stop sooner or later.

They did indeed stop a month or so later. But he continued to feel uneasy. There was someone out there who had a grudge against him, who wanted to harm him.

More worrying was the death threat he received. Someone telephoned the factory to say that he would be dead within a week. The call was anonymous. It had been repeated three times. Dick then received an anonymous letter containing the same message.

For some time he could not think straight. It felt like a bad dream. A British consular official in Bombay had been shot in his car a few weeks earlier. But Dick wondered why any terrorist organisation would want to kill him. When he reported the death threat to the police, they did not take it very seriously. They gave him a retired police officer as a bodyguard for a time and advised him to be careful! In fact, no-one tried to kill him. Things gradually returned to normal. But it was an unnerving experience.

In the meantime, Dick kept Vish under tight control. First of all, he made sure that Vish was kept out of any business connected with the Hosur factory construction project. Dick himself took direct charge of the project, and checked every detail of the contracts. He cancelled the contract with Naveen Construction and re-negotiated a new contract with a company Vish had no connections with. And now that he knew for certain that Vish was dishonest, Dick systematically checked on Vish's other activities. Perhaps Lennox might change his mind if there was sufficient evidence against Vish.

Once they realised that Dick was determined to investigate Vish, some of the other senior staff quietly gave him information and hints about where to look. Dick soon discovered that Vish routinely used company drivers (and company cars) and factory workers to carry out work on his own house, to run errands and to act as waiters at the many parties he gave. He remembered recognising staff at that first dinner party at the Visvanathans' house in Kalakshetra. Dick held another stormy disciplinary meeting with Vish, at which he gave him a formal letter warning him not to exploit staff outside working hours.

Dick then looked into the procedures for disposing of office equipment, such as air-conditioners, typewriters and office furniture. As he had suspected, he found that Vish was selling these at below-market prices to his friends, who then paid the difference directly back to Vish. Dick put a stop to this.

He investigated the system of awarding maintenance contracts for the buildings and machinery. Again, Vish was arranging for these contracts to go to his friends and business associates, with a percentage payment to himself 'under the table'.

It seemed that everywhere Dick looked there was something shady going on; that every stone he turned over had a snake under it!

*   *   *

Every January, the managers of Trakton's Indian factories were called to Delhi for an annual conference and their performance for the year was reviewed. As he did every year, Dick flew up from Madras to Delhi the day before the conference began. He arrived in the early evening. There was a wintry haze over Delhi, partly caused by traffic pollution and partly by the many fires on street corners. Men wrapped in blankets and shawls huddled around these fires as his car passed. On one intersection, near Claridges Hotel, a group of bedraggled, red-uniformed bandsmen waited to be hired for a wedding. A sad-looking, white horse snuffled the dust, in search of grass to eat, while its owners prayed for a bridegroom to ride it.[10]

He was staying as usual at the Imperial Hotel, on Janpath,[11] splendidly unchanged by modern fashions. He was welcomed there in style. A turbaned porter took hold of his bags and whisked him off to a comfortably old-fashioned, spacious, airy room on the ground floor. Dick would never understand the attraction of modern five-star hotels, when such genuine comfort was available. A few moments later the porter returned with a letter. Dick sat down and read it quickly at first, and then more slowly, trying to take it in. The letter was from Lennox.

Dear Dick,

We're all so looking forward to seeing you here in Delhi again. Plenty of issues to discuss, as you'll see from the enclosed agenda.

I think we'd better organise our annual appraisal interview slightly differently this year. There are some difficult issues to be dealt with, especially on the personnel management side. In view of your long association with the company, I don't want to rush to any conclusions but clearly I have to keep the company's best interests in mind. To keep things confidential, I think it's better to do this outside the office. I suggest therefore, that we meet for a business breakfast at my place the morning after the conference is over. It will give us a better chance to discuss your future. You'll be away in time to take the early afternoon flight to Madras, so no problem there.

Barbara and I look forward to seeing you for drinks this evening along with the others.

Yours, as ever,
Keith.

At seven, a company car collected him and took him off to Keith's house, just off Aurangzeb Road opposite Claridges Hotel. Most of his colleagues had already arrived.

He felt strangely uneasy. The letter, with its combination of forced friendliness and concealed threat ('keep things confidential', 'I have to keep the company's best interests in mind') had unnerved him. He felt insecure, even among these people he had known and worked with for years. Cameron Laidlaw from the Calcutta office joked with him about their entry into middle age. Was this a veiled suggestion that he was getting too old for his job? Jim Prentice from Bombay talked enthusiastically about the latest management systems. Was this a hint that Dick was somehow falling behind the latest trends? Frank Prendergast from Kanpur talked darkly about 'major re-structuring'. Did this mean some senior jobs would soon be lost? And Keith himself constantly referred to the 'generation gap' and the need to 'update'. Was this an indirect criticism of the more experienced staff?

By the time they sat down to dinner Dick had drunk more than was wise. By the end of the dinner he felt the floating sensation which he knew was a danger signal. He excused himself – and left, staggering slightly as he made his way to the car.

*   *   *

The two-day conference went well. All the factories had had an exceptionally good year and profits were soaring. But throughout the conference there were ambiguous remarks about the future and conspiratorial looks between those sitting round the table. Dick wondered what was going on below the calm surface of the meeting.

Or was it just his imagination?

The morning after the conference, Dick went for a walk in the garden around Humayun's Tomb. Even at seven in the morning there was plenty of activity: overweight women in track suits jogging heavily in the frosty dawn light – hoping to cancel out the overeating of the coming day with a little gentle physical exercise; respectable gentlemen in woollen scarves walking their dogs; students training in the chill of the dawn. And all of this in the looming shadow of the great crumbling domes of the Mughal emperor's mausoleum,[12] mysterious in the misty air.

By half past eight Dick was in the dining room at South End Road. Keith's wife Barbara had welcomed him, looking fresh and bright as usual. She was a 'comfortable' woman, completely devoted to making her husband happy. She spent most of her time and energy on her home and on cooking, for which she was justly famous. Everyone enjoyed Barbara's home-made cakes, her pies, her soufflés, her barbecued fish ... She was not a very stimulating person to talk to, unless the subject was cooking, gardening, interior decoration or babies. But everyone liked her for her simple kindness, and for her tact. In spite of her position as the boss's wife, she never made anyone feel small or unimportant.

After a few minutes of polite conversation with Barbara, Keith appeared. Barbara then tactfully left them alone together and went upstairs.

'Tea or coffee?' asked Keith politely, the perfect host. Dick wondered uneasily if this was the condemned man's breakfast.

'Coffee thanks. But can we get on with the interview, Keith? I'm a bit confused by your decision to hold it here.'

'No hurry, Dick. Let's just enjoy our breakfast first, shall we?' And he took a large mouthful of bacon and freshly fried egg as he spoke.

Dick had no appetite for the food but he managed to chew his way silently through it. When they had finished they moved, with a last cup of coffee, into Keith's study. It was a room designed to impress visitors, with framed photographs of Keith with the President of the Republic, Keith with the Queen, Keith with the Minister of Trade and Industry. The bookshelves were lined with the latest books on management, and a state-of-the-art personal computer stood on his desk.

'Right, Dick. Let me come to the point as quickly as possible. The company is doing well. But, to keep ahead of the competition, we have to bring in new people and make sure that we are absolutely top quality on the management side.'

'Of course,' Dick replied, 'but surely last year's results show that we have been doing just that?'

'Well, up to a point, you're right of course,' said Keith, with a slightly embarrassed smile, 'but we mustn't forget the personnel management side.'

'What do you mean by that?' asked Dick warily.

'Well, the thing is, I've been getting rather a lot of complaints about the way things are going in the Madras factory. Experienced local staff under-appreciated, that sort of thing. Problems with the new factory project in Hosur. Friction with the senior management, you know. People feeling they are undervalued.'

'No. I don't know,' said Dick, feeling his anger rising. 'In fact, it's simply not true.'

'Well, opinions obviously differ on that, as far as I can tell. I've also had to warn you about not doing anything to endanger the company's position in India, if you remember,' Keith continued. Dick had to forcibly stop himself from making an angry response.

'What I've called you here to consider, Dick, is the possibility of you taking early retirement. As you know, the company makes very generous retirement arrangements for senior staff. My own feeling is that you need a change. To be absolutely frank, you haven't taken advantage of all the management training schemes we've offered you either. You've done pretty well everywhere you've been for the company, but times are changing Dick – you can't go on in the old style for ever. You can't simply rely on your past achievements – we have to look to the future. I really do think you should give this offer your serious consideration.' He paused for effect. 'It might not come again.'

Dick felt the scarcely-concealed threat in those words.

'I'll certainly consider it,' Dick said grimly, 'but I can't guarantee I'll accept. I'll need to talk to Sally anyway. But I just don't understand why you should be pushing me to take retirement when the Madras results are the best of all our factories in India.'

'Well, as your manager, you must understand that I have to look at the wider picture. I can't really say more, Dick. I hope you understand what I'm telling you.'

It was ten before Dick left, feeling betrayed and shaken by the interview. They had wrestled verbally over everything but Keith had refused to change his position. Dick felt that Keith had not told him honestly what the problem was but the sinister reference to Keith's earlier warning, about Vish, was worrying. He continued to go over the interview in his mind for the rest of the day – and for long after it.

Despite Keith's assurances, Dick's flight to Madras was delayed by the notorious winter fog in Delhi. It was past midnight when he eventually arrived in Madras. During the drive from the airport back to his home he dozed in an unpleasant half-sleep, barely noticing the stray cattle and water buffaloes wandering across the path of the car.

When he arrived home, Sally had already gone to bed. He went to his study and poured himself a large glass of whisky. There were letters for him on his desk. He tore open a large envelope, with the company logo on it, marked 'Personal: in Confidence'. It contained details of the early retirement scheme. But this was clearly not an offer; it was an order. He had no choice. Obviously all the decisions had already been taken before his interview with Lennox. The envelope also contained the copy of a letter to Jim Mann, appointing Jim to the Madras factory to take over Dick's job in one month's time.

He poured himself another glass of whisky. He felt angry – at the injustice, at the hypocrisy of Keith, who had not had the courage to tell him the whole truth – and then depressed, as he thought about his own loss of self-respect, his stupidity at having trusted 'old friends'. He felt betrayed. He had worked for Trakton for twenty-five years, had sacrificed his first wife to it and a gaping emptiness now faced him. His whole life had been built around a company that had just decided to throw him out for no good reason. There now seemed very little to live for.

It was five before he eventually dragged himself to bed. The empty bottle stood on the desk, the only witness to his agony.

Chapter 4   *Break-up and breakdown: November 1989*

With nothing to keep them in India any longer, Dick and Sally returned to England and moved back into their house in Cambridge. It was a big comfortable house on the edge of the city which they had bought many years earlier, and only used occasionally, for holidays; the rest of the time it had been rented to visiting professors from abroad. It was the nearest thing they had to a home – but still it felt unfamiliar, somehow temporary.

For a time Dick made an effort to re-adjust to life in Cambridge. They joined a film club, visited the theatre regularly, gave one or two small parties in an attempt to re-establish contact with old friends. Dick even had dinner in his old college once but found the social atmosphere so chilly, the conversation so boring and the food so indigestible that he decided not to repeat the experience. He even offered his services as a lecturer at evening classes in business administration – but there were no vacancies.

Dick quickly realised that he no longer felt at home in Britain. It was also clear to him that he had no real friends left in England and that his sense of purpose had been destroyed when he lost his job. He tried not to feel bitter, but it was difficult. Gradually he sank into an aimless existence, sleeping late, reading the newspapers till midday, then going down to the local pub for a few pints of beer and a sandwich.

For Sally, it was different. She fitted back into Britain as if she had never left it. She slipped effortlessly into a social life he had never shared anyway. She found part-time work in a local charity organisation. She had a role. He realised that she belonged here, whereas he did not – not any more.

They shared less and less. He broke off relations with his daughter Angie over an argument about how she should bring up her children. Angie and her husband believed in giving their children total freedom. This was not the way Dick had been brought up. Neither was it the way he had raised Angie herself. During a visit to their house, they argued and Dick stormed out of the house. He never visited them again.

He also argued with his son Simon about his wife Melanie. Dick could not stand Melanie and insulted her in front of Simon. Neither Simon nor Sally ever forgave him.

He had isolated himself from his wife and his children; now he felt isolated even from himself.

Sally spent more and more time out of the house; Dick spent more and more time in it. He began to drink heavily. Sally would return at five in the evening to find him drunk. She began to come back later, hoping to find him in bed. He usually was – snoring noisily.

They spoke little to each other and, when they did, it was only to talk about everyday practical matters – who would get petrol for the car, what they would buy at the supermarket, when the bills had to be paid, when the tax returns were due. It was only occasionally that Dick felt able to speak about his inner feelings of hopelessness and despair.

'I know you think I'm exaggerating,' he began, one

Sunday morning over breakfast, 'I know we're well off, my pension is more than enough to live on, we don't have to worry about money, we have a nice house, Cambridge is a dream city ... I know all that. But can't you understand that I have lost my sense of purpose?'

'All I can say is that you'd better find another one then,' Sally replied, not very sympathetically.

'It's easy enough for you to say that, but I can't focus my mind any more. I feel as if I can't do anything useful any more. No-one needs me any more. You've got your life. The kids have theirs – and anyway I've spoiled things there too. The company was my life. I don't seem to be able to find anything else worthwhile to do.'

'Well, one thing you could certainly do is drink less. To be honest, I think you're pathetic. You're just wallowing in self-pity. Just think of all the other managers and executives who've lost their jobs and been thrown out on the street, with mortgages to pay, and their kids to bring up – and with no compensation at all. For Christ's sake, Dick, stop feeling so sorry for yourself. Pull yourself together and find something to occupy your mind.'

This conversation was repeated, with variations, at intervals over the next few months. In July they went on holiday to Spain, but it was ruined by Dick's drunken behaviour and Sally's frozen silences. It was a depressing experience for both of them. The night after their return, their simmering rage against each other broke through the surface. Dick was opening a bottle of wine when it slipped from his hands and smashed on the kitchen floor. Their tension splintered along with the bottle.

'You bloody drunk!' screamed Sally. 'Can't you even

open a bottle now? I don't think I can stand this any more. You fall into bed stinking of drink. You can't behave politely with anyone. Your children can't stand you. And you lie around feeling sorry for yourself from morning till night. What are you for God's sake? You make me sick. Sick, sick, sick ... I'm going to bed. You can do what you like, you pathetic bastard, but don't wake me up with your moaning!'

Dick smashed his glass against the wall, took the car keys and drove into town. After a few desperate drinks and dinner in the Riverside Restaurant, he began to feel that things were not so bad after all. Sally had exploded before. It was true that he was drinking a bit too much. He decided to cut down on drinking. Perhaps he should join a health club. Things could be put right between them. Sally was a good woman. She would understand him better if he made an effort. She would appreciate that. The alcohol made him feel optimistic.

He left the restaurant and stumbled unsteadily along the towpath next to the river. He recalled the days when he had walked here as an undergraduate. Who could have predicted what his life would become? He stood swaying for a moment on the river bank. A plane was passing over, high in the sky overhead. He raised his head to look at it, lost his balance, slipped and tumbled into the river.

A group of Japanese tourists pulled him out of the water. In fact, he had fallen in at a place where the water was only half a metre deep – but very muddy! He could not find his car keys. No taxi would agree to drive him home, so he had had to stagger the mile or so back home on foot, his wet, muddy clothes sticking uncomfortably to his skin. On arrival, he discovered that he had lost his house key too. Sally opened the door to find a stinking, muddy husband on the doorstep. She said nothing until the following morning.

'I'm sorry Dick, but we can't go on like this,' she said at breakfast. 'I've tried to be patient with you. I do understand that you've been injured by what's happened. But I just can't stand it any longer. I don't recognise you any more. You're not the man I married. You've become a total stranger. The only thing is for us to separate, at least for a time. Either you leave or I do. You decide. Please sleep in the guest bedroom tonight. I shall be out all day today. We'll speak again tomorrow morning.'

But by the time Dick got out of bed the next morning it was eleven o'clock. Sally had gone out. He packed his clothes, some personal papers and his laptop computer into two cases. He called his sister Maureen in Reading to ask if he could stay for a day or two. He wrote a short note to Sally. Then he called a cab and left the house in Long Road. He knew he would never return to it.

Chapter 5   *Down at Hove*

The grey waves sucked at the stony beach. The horizon was a misty blur. Dick walked along the seafront into a stiff, cold wind. Spray from the sea mixed with icy rain lashed his face. It was only three in the afternoon but the sky was already dark. Soon it would be evening, then night – another endless night to be spent alone.

He made his way unsteadily back to his small flat in George Square. The square was impressive. The grand Regency-style houses took up three sides of it; the fourth was open to the sea. A public garden occupied the centre. His flat was on the third floor. It comprised a living room, a bedroom, a study, a small kitchen which smelt of old cooking oil and a tiny bathroom with noisy plumbing. It was cramped and depressing. But it was anonymous, and it was cheap. Dick had rented it from a friend of his sister Maureen, soon after leaving Sally three months previously.

As autumn turned slowly to winter in Hove, Dick's despair grew deeper. The days were a succession of self-hatred, drinking and nightmare sleep. Each morning he woke at four, then struggled to find sleep again. By the time dawn came he had fallen into a deep slumber, and only woke again at eleven.

He got into the habit of taking lunch in a cheap Spanish restaurant, on the high street. They served an oily paella with a red house wine which tasted like anti-freeze fluid. The main attraction was the waitresses, who were young and attractive and obviously available for other services if required. He had only once invited one of them back to his sad flat. He decided not to repeat the experiment. Sex without commitment was not his style.

After lunch he would take his walk along the seafront, gloomy in its winter mood. The sea was always grey or brown, almost always rough and threatening. The sad hotels and boarding houses sulked in the winter light. Hove was a forlorn mixture of the genteel and the shabby; of retired civil servants and unemployed teenagers.

In the afternoons he tried to write. At first he had thought about writing his memoirs. He quickly realised that no-one would be interested in reading them. He then began writing poetry. It was intensely personal, it was confused – it was certainly not likely to be published. But, in some ways, it kept him from going mad.

In the evenings he would drink steadily until he fell into a deep sleep. More than once he woke in the middle of the night to find himself still slumped in his armchair. The days were a blur, lacking any focus, any purpose, anything to look forward to.

*   *   *

He rarely received anything through the post except advertisements and bills. But one morning he was surprised to find a letter with an Indian stamp on it. Sally had sent it on from Cambridge. He recognised the neat handwriting as Ramu's.

Ramu (short for Ramanathan) had been his personal assistant in Madras; a sort of secretary, advisor and confidant rolled into one. He had also become a good friend.

Dear Dick,

I hope all is well with you and with family members also. I have been worrying a little because we have not been hearing from you for some time now. Suresh and others have been asking of you also. Please send us your news soon to relieve our worries.

I am fine but I have been transferred by Mr Mann to Registry. It seems he prefers someone recommended by Vish as an assistant. I wonder why? Otherwise things are running much the same way. The factory is doing well – but the Hosur factory project has been suspended: something to do with changing contractors – but management does not tell us what. There is a rumour that Vish is re-negotiating the contract with some other company. That will be interesting, will it not? People also say that Mr Lennox will soon be returning to London on promotion.

You remember Nagarajan in the Accounts department? You helped him out when his wife died. Well, he has also taken 'early retirement' and gone back to his hometown near Bangalore. He is a broken man.

All along I have suspected something but now I am sure. The reason you and Nagarajan were sent on early retirement is definitely some sort of plot of Vish and Molly's. They somehow persuaded Lennox to get rid of you. How do I know this? I will tell you.

Number 1: Before you went to Delhi that last time, Molly had also gone. She said that she was on sick leave but I have found on the file the receipt for the air ticket. In Central

Filing we can discover many things! I checked with Pal in the Delhi office and he remembers seeing her in Lennox's office at about that time.

Number 2: I have also overheard some interesting conversations. One day I heard Vish threatening Nambiar in Accounts. 'You do what I told you, or I'll arrange for you to take early retirement too.'

On another occasion I overheard Molly telling one of her friends that Mr Mann was not like you – he knew how to behave himself. He had 'learnt his lesson' from what had happened to you, she said.

Number 3: I have also obtained a personal note from Lennox to Vish. Don't ask me how I came by it. In Central Filing you can sometimes find things which ought to have been destroyed. Anyway, it is obviously about you. It agrees with Vish that 'something has to be done urgently' because you were getting too curious, especially about the Hosur factory project. I will show it to you one day if you wish.

What does all this mean? It means that they were all in it together. It means that they all wanted you out of the way. Maybe you can understand why but it is not yet clear to me. Anyway I thought you should know about it, in case you can make some sense of it. I hope I have done the correct thing by informing you of same.

I will write another letter when I hear from you. All your friends here join me in sending very sincere greetings to Sally and to your good self.

Yours,
Ramu.

The letter was dated 15 October, so it had taken some

time to arrive. Dick made himself a cup of coffee and took it to the big window overlooking the square. It was raining, and a lone traffic warden sticking fines on parked cars was the only sign of human life.

Dick read the letter again, then re-read it. He sat reflecting on its contents, thinking back to the time of his 'retirement'. He forgot to go out for lunch, and it was three in the afternoon before he got up from his desk. He grabbed his coat and went out for a long walk along the seafront.

He felt he was thinking more clearly than he had for months. The letter had confirmed all of his suspicions and, as he walked, his thoughts were a mixture of happiness and anger. He was happy that he still had some friends back in India and angry that he was right about the connection between the Visvanathans and Lennox.

His thoughts then turned to revenge, and by the time he returned to the flat, his mind was made up: he would find out what lay behind the relationship between Lennox and the Visvanathans, and make it public.

Chapter 6   *Return to Madras*

By the beginning of December 1989, Dick had made arrangements to return to Madras. He would be leaving on 15 December. Ramu had reserved a room for him at the Madras Club. Since receiving Ramu's letter, Dick had become more like his old self. He was taking regular exercise and had almost stopped drinking. He felt a new sense of energy. He had a purpose again. And now he was returning to a place he loved and where he felt at home.

He had also reached some decisions about his life. On the evening before he left, he called Sally to tell her that he had seen a lawyer about their divorce. The conversation was civilised and polite, but distant. Both of them knew that their relationship was over for ever but neither could quite believe it. He explained the financial arrangements he had made and told her he would be away in India for a month or two. She did not ask him why he was going. As he put the telephone down, he felt that a chapter of his life had ended, quickly followed by excitement at the prospect of a new start.

It was early morning as the plane circled over St Thomas' Mount and landed with a nasty bump on the runway at Madras. Two hours later Dick finally cleared immigration, collected his case from the squeaking baggage conveyor-belt, and made his way through customs, unchallenged by the fierce-looking uniformed officers.

Outside the sun was up, and as he passed from the air-conditioned cool of the baggage hall into the sunlight, he was met by a wave of steamy heat, pungent with the first smell of India – a mixture of spices and diesel fumes.

Ramu had arranged a car to meet him. Fighting his way through the crowd of beggars and boys trying to grab his suitcase from him, Dick climbed into the back of the battered old Ambassador. The driver was a thin little man with skin the colour of coal dust, who said nothing but who wove his way skilfully in and out of the chaos of the morning rush-hour to the calm of the Madras Club.

Dick was pleased to find a note from Paul Fernando, the Anglo-Indian manager of the club, inviting him for an evening pre-dinner drink. Courtesy was not yet dead – at least not in southern India.

His room, in the guest wing, was spacious, with a high ceiling, a large ceiling fan which swooped through the sticky air, slicing it into cooler segments, a bed fitted with a mosquito net, and an antique writing desk. The bathroom was almost as large as the bedroom; old-fashioned but with a shower which worked. The rooms had all the luxury of simplicity.

After a lengthy shower, he called room service for a cold beer and sat with it on the balcony looking towards the Adyar River. There were magnificent tamarinds and raintrees, umbrellas of shade for the green parakeets, doves and mynahs. The club was an eighteenth-century building, formerly the residence of the Anglican Bishop of Madras. It was a splendid white building, with a dome and large columns at the entrance. It overlooked the Adyar River, which was an impressive view, provided it was seen from a distance. Seen closer up, it was a sluggish channel of evil-smelling, black, polluted water – an ecological disaster.

After lunch, he called some of his closer friends, in particular Ramu and Suresh. They agreed to meet at the Raintree Restaurant in the Connemara Hotel the following evening.

The Connemara was one of the oldest hotels in the city. The Raintree Restaurant was tucked away in a garden area at the rear of the main hotel. It served Chettiar[13] food, spicy but sophisticated – a complex range of flavours which exploded in the mouth one after the other.

Ramu and Suresh were waiting for him in the lobby. When they reached the table, he found Lalitha and Nirupama too ... A nice surprise. Conversation, most of it about the most recent gossip and scandal, got under way immediately. Noshir Battliwallah had been discovered in the bed of the American Consul-General's wife. Nicky Patel was having a homosexual affair with the son of a State Minister. The daughter of a leading doctor had run off, temporarily, with a press photographer ... There was no lack of material!

Over coffee, conversation turned to the Visvanathans. They went back over the long history of their misdeeds. How Vish had been involved in a bank fraud case way back in 1970 – and how Keith Lennox had given evidence for him in court, and how Vish had been let off. How he had organised alcohol smuggling in the early 1980s before Dick had arrived. How he had repeatedly cheated the company over the resale of air-conditioners and other surplus equipment. How the Visvanathans had regularly exploited junior staff, using them as unpaid personal servants at their home. How they had arranged a system of under-the-table payments for the award of contracts. The list went on and on. The Visvanathans had done very well out of their position.

But questions still needed to be answered: how had they got away with it for such a long period? And why should they have been considered dangerous to the company? It made no sense. Surely it should have been easy just to get rid of them? Why had no-one done it?

One new thing which Dick learnt was that Molly had been away for a year in the UK in 1970. This was very unusual, and no-one knew why she had been given permission to go. Immediately after her return, she and Vish had announced the date of their marriage. It had attracted attention at the time because Vish was a Hindu Brahmin,[14] and Molly a Keralite[15] Christian, and the fact that they had hardly known each other before Molly went away so suddenly in 1970. They never had any children.

Dick also wanted to find out what had happened to Nagarajan. Nagarajan had been in charge of Accounts at Trakton when Dick left. He had been closely involved in the Hosur factory project. Suresh gave Dick his address in Devanahalli.

'I don't know exactly what he knows – but I'm sure he knows something. And he likes you. He always used to talk about how you helped him out when his wife died. Maybe it will help if you take a bottle when you visit him. Anyway, if anyone can help you, I'm sure he can.'

Chapter 7   *Nagarajan*

It was not till after Christmas that Dick managed to establish contact with Nagarajan. His letters went unanswered and the telephone number Suresh had given him rang engaged the whole time. Dick spent the Christmas and New Year holiday looking up old friends. Eventually he received a card from Nagarajan, inviting him to visit 'at your earliest convenience'.

Dick took the early morning flight to Bangalore and checked into the West End Hotel, his favourite hotel in the whole of India. It was still an island of peace in a city which had gone wild with development. The rooms were in separate buildings surrounded with gardens and trees. The service was efficient and polite, and the rooms comfortable and spacious.

It took Dick some time to get through to the number in Devanahalli. Nagarajan eventually came to the phone. He sounded vague and confused, but the line crackled so badly that Dick could not really tell. He managed to communicate his message – that he would be coming over to Devanahalli the next morning. Nagarajan told him he would be welcome.

Dick took an early breakfast on the terrace of the West End. He ordered idlis[16] with masala[17] and chutney[18] – and the jet-black southern Indian filter coffee. The grass in the garden was wet with dew, and he wrapped himself tighter in his Kashmiri shawl to keep warm. There had been a wedding party in the garden the night before; now the grass was littered with fading orange marigold garlands[19] and bruised jasmine[20] flowers turning from white to brown. He wondered how long the newly-married couple's happiness would last. He hoped it would be longer than the brief beauty of these flowers.

He hired a car with a driver for the day, and by eight they were threading their way through the morning rush hour towards the northern exit from the city. Under the British Raj,[21] Bangalore had been an army town with wide tree-lined roads and comfortable bungalows. It was still an important military base. But now it was also the high-tech capital of India, with space industries, aeronautics, computer software, telecommunications, silicon chips – the works. The bungalows were being rapidly replaced by high-rise blocks, shopping malls and luxury apartments. And it now had the worst traffic pollution Dick had experienced for years.

They passed the Maharajah's palace, hidden behind groves of eucalyptus trees. Then out beyond the Agricultural College and all the research institutes which were springing up along the road. They passed the Parsee 'Towers of Silence' where dead bodies were left exposed to be eaten by birds of prey. It looked abandoned and did not seem to have been used for some time.

The traffic was chaotic: yellow auto-rickshaws weaving in and out of the traffic, sometimes carrying seven or more people; buses so overloaded that they sagged down at one corner; lorries piled so high with sugarcane that they seemed about to turn over; old cars driven by even older men clutching the steering wheel as if their lives depended on it (and they did!). Gradually the traffic thinned as they got farther from the city.

Rural India, the India of the villages, surrounded them again very soon after they left the city. Bullock carts moved slowly along, loaded with sugarcane, hay, groups of people. The road was lined with tamarind trees, many of them scarred by traffic accidents, and with families of monkeys playing under them. Beside the road there were the dark green mango orchards, fields of grapevines, groves of coconut palms, silvery sugarcane plantations, small fields of red peppers. And of course the bare granite rock of the Deccan Plateau.

They turned right at the road junction at Dodballapur, taking the direction of Nandi Hills. Dick had heard about the Hills but never visited them. He did not realise then what an important role they were to play in his life.

It was ten when they arrived in Devanahalli. It took some time before Shaukat, the driver, located Nagarajan's house. They found it in a quiet lane, well away from the town centre. It was a single-storey house, built from granite blocks, like all the other houses in the town. It was built around a courtyard, in the traditional southern Indian style. Nagarajan was waiting for Dick at the entrance.

*   *   *

Dick was shocked when he saw Nagarajan. He was like a dried-up plant: brown and lifeless. They went into the courtyard of the house. Sitting in a shady corner, they began to talk. Nagarajan's daughter, Lakshmi, served them coffee.

When Dick first saw Lakshmi he felt he instantly

42

recognised her, although he had never met her before. It was as if he had always known her. She was in her early thirties, or so he guessed. Her skin was dark, much darker than Nagarajan's, with a warm glow. It was her eyes which caught his attention first – dark pools in which her feelings surfaced. Her long, jet-black hair hung down her back. She wore a simple sari[22] which did not completely hide the outline of her full breasts and narrow waist. She moved with an indefinable grace. She was, quite simply, the most beautiful woman he had ever seen. Their eyes met briefly before she bent to pour the coffee.

While Lakshmi busied herself with preparing lunch, Nagarajan told Dick that she was a widow. He had arranged her marriage to a boy from the same community, a computer software specialist. They had married at the boy's home town, near Udipi in North Karnataka, when she was twenty-two. By then she had completed her MA[23] in English literature. It was time for babies, grandchildren to warm the old people's hearts, and to justify their years of work and struggle. But no children came. And, five years later Girijan, her husband, had died in a motorcycle accident. She had returned to her father and now took care of him in his retirement. That was the only role left to her.

As they talked, Nagarajan drank. Dick had brought him a bottle of duty-free whisky as a present. Nagarajan steadily drank his way through it. He had always been a heavy cigarette smoker but now he smoked beedies; thin, hand-rolled, black tobacco sticks which gave off an acrid smoke and choked anyone who inhaled it. The room was soon filled with smoke.

'The horse races begin again soon,' he said, coughing his

dry smoker's cough. 'I've got some good tips for winners this season. I could certainly use some extra money. The company pension is miserable. Look at this place.' He gestured around him at the room they sat in, with its cement floor and bare stone walls. 'I always knew there was something funny with that bitch Molly,' he said, abruptly changing the subject. 'It was her who got me sacked you know. Her and her bastard of a husband. They didn't like the questions I was asking about the Hosur factory contract. Somehow they got to Lennox with stories about me – unreliable, dishonest (me, dishonest!), interfering, inefficient and all that. So, one morning, not long after you'd gone, I got this letter. I'd been given early retirement, just like you. Only I got the minimum payment. There was nothing I could do about it. I wrote letters to Delhi but never got a proper answer. What the hell was going on there, Dick?'

'I'd hoped you might tell me,' said Dick. 'How is it that the Visvanathans always seemed to have so much power?'

'I don't know for sure, Dick,' said Nagarajan, becoming more and more informal as the whisky took its effect. (He had never before called Dick by his first name!)

'But you know that they all knew each other in the old days, don't you? Madras was Lennox's first post with the company. I remember because I'd only just joined as a typist. Vish was a typist, like me, and Molly was a telephone operator.

That Molly was quite a girl in those days. She knew how to enjoy herself all right. Plenty of rumours about her, I can tell you. I think old Ned, Ned Outram, he was in the factory at the time as Chief Engineer; I think old Ned

44

fancied her. They went out together I think, for a while. I'm pretty sure it was Ned. I don't know, it's all mixed up in my mind now. Lennox was around too, without his wife to start with. She only came out to join him later. It was all such a long time ago. It wasn't long after that that she went off to the UK on special leave – Molly I mean. That caused some gossip, I can tell you. She told everyone she was going to look after her sick uncle in Birmingham. No-one believed that though. Some people even said she'd gone to have an abortion in secret. I don't know about that, but I know she didn't waste any time in marrying Vish when she got back. And they never had any children. I always wondered about that. Of course Lennox had gone to Egypt by then – on promotion. I always thought he was a crafty bastard, that one. Was it Ned? I don't know. Have another drink, Dick.'

'Doesn't anyone know what she really did when she was in the UK?' asked Dick. 'Surely someone must know.'

'Maybe Percy Hancock might know, if he's still alive. He was in charge in Delhi at that time. He must have approved the leave. I always thought they were perfectly suited to each other – Molly and Vish I mean. Both as evil as each other. I hate their guts. I just hope they get their punishment one day. Have another drink . . .'

Nagarajan's confused conversation was interrupted when Lakshmi brought them lunch. It was simple vegetarian food – rice, dal[24] and vegetable masala with chappaties[25] – but the aroma was delicious. Lakshmi, in traditional Indian style, did not eat with them – she would eat later. Dick ate hungrily but Nagarajan only picked at his food while continuing to smoke yet another beedie. As soon as the meal was over, Nagarajan excused himself and tottered unsteadily across the courtyard to his room for an afternoon sleep, leaving Dick alone at the table.

*   *   *

It was some time before Lakshmi returned to clear the dishes. She said nothing and went about her work with her eyes lowered, not looking at Dick. As she was about to leave the room, Dick asked her, 'How is your father? What has happened to him?'

'As you can see,' she said, 'he has lost hope in life. It has happened since he retired. My mother died the same year. He has not forgiven himself, though he was not to blame. Now he drinks quite a bit; it helps him remember the good times. He often speaks of you. He has never forgotten what you did to help when my mother was so ill – before all this happened.'

She spoke softly but in a dark, warm voice that sent a tremor through Dick. He did not want her to leave the room.

'How long have you been with him here?'

'Just over a year now, since my husband was killed.'

'Your father told me. I am so sorry. It must be very difficult for you.'

She raised her eyes to look straight at him. There were no tears but they seemed full of hidden suffering.

'It was an arranged marriage. We never, how can I explain ...? What has happened, has happened. It cannot be changed. Many people are less fortunate than me.'

'But don't you get lonely here with only your father for company?'

'I am not lonely. It is not hard work to look after my

46

father. As you can see, he eats little. He is often out of the house. I have time to think ... and to read. I read a lot. Books are good company. In any case they are what I have.'

He was about to ask another question – anything to keep her with him for a few more minutes – when she suddenly changed the subject.

'You must be feeling tired after your journey. I will show you the guest room. You can take a sleep too. My father will not wake until teatime.'

Their eyes met briefly before she led him across the courtyard to the room next to her father's.

'Enjoy your rest. I will call you at teatime.' She turned away from him and walked slowly back across the courtyard.

He lay on the bed. His thoughts were confused; Molly and her mysterious year in Britain, Nagarajan's dead existence in this small town, his own sudden fascination for Lakshmi. The thoughts came and went, moved in and out of focus. If only, he thought ...

He was woken by a gentle knocking and Lakshmi's voice, 'If you are ready, I am serving tea to my father in five minutes.'

*   *   *

Tea was an uncomfortable experience. Nagarajan's mood seemed to be heavy without alcohol to lighten it. (The whisky bottle now stood empty on the table.) He still seemed half-asleep. He silently smoked one beedie after another while slowly sipping his tea. Lakshmi said nothing, though Dick occasionally caught her eye. After drinking two cups, Dick rose to leave.

'Why don't you stay?' asked Nagarajan, roughly. 'Isn't

my house good enough for you?' Lakshmi opened her mouth to speak but he silenced her with a look. 'Anyway, I thought you would stay for one or two days. There's no-one to talk to here except fools.' He seemed unaware of the insult to his own daughter, but no doubt she did not qualify as someone fit to have a conversation with.

'Anyway, go if you must. But you're always welcome to my house. I've never forgotten what you did for Mrs Nagarajan. Ask Percy Hancock. He must know something.'

Dick left him slumped in an old chair in the corner of the darkening room, still smoking. The sound of his cough followed Dick out. Lakshmi accompanied him to the door leading to the street. His car was waiting. They stood for a moment before he got in.

'Please excuse my father for his rudeness. He doesn't mean it. It's the way he is now. It's not always easy to ... ' Her voice trembled as she looked down. He saw the tears filling her eyes.

'There's nothing to excuse,' said Dick. 'I've had a good day and you've been very hospitable. I think I shall take your father up on his offer to come again.'

'I hope you will.' Her voice was steady again and she smiled.

As the car drove off, he looked back. She was still standing in the street. She did not wave. Behind her, rising above the town, he saw the dark shape of the Nandi Hills in the gathering dusk.

Chapter 8   *Cambridge, February 1990*

'Hello, old chap. Do come in. Have a seat. How about a glass of sherry? Or would you prefer something stronger? Dry or sweet? Dry. Fine. Me too. Nothing like a glass of old Fino is there? Good for the soul I always say. My goodness though, long time no see, isn't it?'

Now knighted,[26] Sir Percy Hancock, former Chief Executive of Trakton, and before that Head of the Delhi office of the company, sank back into his leather armchair, sherry glass in hand, eyes twinkling behind his half-moon spectacles. Dick guessed that what he meant by 'long time no see' was – 'What the hell have you come to see me about after all these years? I smell a rat. What are you trying to get out of me?'

Sir Percy was well-known for his charm. He was the son of a baronet,[27] had been educated at Eton and Trinity College, Cambridge, had a distinguished record with the Guards[28] during the Second World War, for which he had been awarded a DSO,[29] had married the daughter of a banker, done very well for himself with Trakton – and was now, a widower, enjoying his sunset years alone in Cambridge. The last thing he wanted was trouble. And, despite his sophisticated, kindly, charming manner, he had a reputation for acting ruthlessly if the occasion demanded it.

But everyone said he also had the memory of an

elephant. That was the key issue for Dick. Would he remember what had gone on in Madras over twenty years earlier? And, even if he did, would he tell Dick what he knew?

Dick had telephoned him, simply saying he would like to see him on a brief visit to Cambridge while carrying out some 'research'. Sir Percy had invited him to lunch; he could hardly have done less for a former colleague.

The Georgian house in Chaucer Road was spacious and comfortable in the English style. There was no sign of modern interior design. The furniture was comfortable rather than stylish. There were antique Persian rugs on the floor. The walls were covered with old pictures of Eton and Cambridge, with framed photographs of Sir Percy's father being introduced to King George V, of Sir Percy with Nehru ... It was not exactly a museum but it had a strong sense of history about it. A long garden stretched away behind the house – equally English, with wide flower beds, flowering trees and perfectly kept grass. Even in winter, there were flowers.

'So what's all this about research, eh? Didn't know you were into the academic stuff. What's it all about then?'

There was a suspicious edge to his voice but he continued to smile.

'Well, it's just that I have plenty of time on my hands now, so I've been thinking of writing a book. I thought I could do a sort of study of economic development in India. I'd use Trakton as a kind of case study. So I'm just collecting some background information, filling in details I'm not familiar with – that sort of thing ... I know you're a real encyclopaedia on the early days of the company, so I thought I'd try to pick your brains – to see if my idea is possible.'

'Not many brains left now, dear boy,' Sir Percy said innocently. 'I say, mustn't let the food get cold. Let's have our lunch. Cooks are so hard to find these days. I'm lucky to have Mrs Dobbs – can't afford to upset her, you know.'

Mrs Dobbs, a large, silent woman in her fifties served them smoked salmon, followed by a delicious meat pie and a lemon sorbet for dessert. They drank Gaillac Perle with the salmon. 'Get it from a chum of mine. Has a vineyard, you know. Not bad, eh?' They also drank a dark red, fruity Cahors with the pie.

'You have to take care of yourself when you're my age,' said Sir Percy, referring to the lunch. 'Regular meals. Good solid food, proper food, none of this junk food, you know. Keep it simple though. Nothing in excess, what? Have another glass to finish off? Never mind, I'll finish it for supper. Good for the blood-pressure, I believe. Let's have some coffee in the study.'

As they sat in the comfortable, book-lined study, Dick realised that Sir Percy had successfully diverted him away from the subject of Trakton all through lunch. He must find a way of getting back to the subject now.

'How long were you with the company in India, sir?' he asked casually.

'Over ten years, dear boy. Over ten years. But of course I don't remember much now. I've lost contact with everyone, you know. No-one has any time for an old fool like me, what? I just look after my garden these days. Are you interested in flowers at all?'

Dick did not reply to this and returned to his questions.

'One of the things I'm hoping to cover in the book is the career profiles of Indian staff – to try to show how office and factory workers became managers – that sort of thing.'

'Rather, dear boy. Good idea.'

Dick decided that he must circle round the subject to confuse Sir Percy, before coming to the point. So he asked Sir Percy about a number of staff from the Delhi headquarters who had done well for themselves as managers. He asked about staff in Bombay, in Calcutta, in Kanpur. Sir Percy talked on and on about what he remembered of them, much of it surprisingly frank and honest. It certainly showed that his memory was as sharp as ever.

Dick swallowed hard and attacked.

'Do you remember the Visvanathans in Madras, sir? Now they did very well.'

'Oh yes. Molly and Vish. I remember sending both of them on training courses at various times, that sort of thing. Excellent material. Splendid. Nice couple too, as I recall. Of course, I didn't know them personally, or anything like that.'

Dick decided to try a daring tactic to surprise Sir Percy. Perhaps it would work. At least it might catch Sir Percy off his guard and make him tell Dick something useful.

'I wonder if you know what happened to Molly Visvanathan's child? The one she had in Britain during her year off. You did know about that, of course? You must have approved her special leave.'

Dick realised with a thrill of excitement that he had accidentally stumbled on the truth. He had hit his target. It was as if a chill suddenly came over the room. Sir Percy had been taken off his guard and for a split second only, he lost his easy, self-assured manner. But, almost at once, he recovered it. When he replied, his voice was as silky and relaxed as ever.

'Yes. Yes, of course. Bad business that, what? Poor gal got in trouble with one of the British staff in Madras, you know. Couldn't have that sort of thing going on. Had to get her away for a bit. She could have stayed on in the UK with the boy but she decided to go back. Named him John I think, yes, John. Gave him her own family name – Verghese.'

'But what became of him? Where is he now? He must be over twenty by now. Does Molly still keep in touch with him?' Dick was anxious to follow up on his unexpected advantage. But Sir Percy was already steering him away from the danger zone.

'Couldn't say, dear boy. Went to a good school and all that. His father paid for it all, as far as I know. Then he came up here I believe. Went to St John's College, if I'm not mistaken. But, I say old boy, I can't see what all this has to do with career development of Indian staff, eh? It was all a long time ago. Better forgotten. There's no point in stirring it all up again. It won't do anyone any good. How about a cognac?'

Dick accepted. They sipped the golden liquid in silence.

'How do you find it, dear boy? It's Armagnac actually. I prefer it. It's got a bit more "oomph" than cognac. Matter of personal taste I suppose.'

Dick nodded appreciatively. He was about to ask his final question, but Sir Percy got in first.

'By the way, there's no point in asking who the father

was. I couldn't possibly tell you that, could I? I'd leave it all alone if I were you, dear boy.'

Dick decided that he would get no more information from Sir Percy, thanked him and left. Sir Percy, elegant in his bow tie and expensive tweeds, walked with him to the gate.

'Take my advice, dear boy. By all means write your book, if that's your intention – but forget about all this Molly business. It could get you into trouble; serious trouble. Do come again, dear boy, when you can spare the time. I've got a really nice Chablis in the cellar I'd like to try on you. Come in the summer when we can sit out and enjoy the garden.'

Chapter 9   *Jacko of St John's*

Dick looked at his watch; half past four already. The lunch had gone on far longer than he'd expected. The old boy certainly had stamina. Dick decided to walk back to St John's, his old college. He would go along the Backs.[30] The frosty February air by the river would help to clear his head.

As he turned down Fen Causeway, he thought again about Sir Percy's reaction to his question about Molly's child. He'd obviously decided there was no point in denying it. That would not have fooled Dick. Instead, he had told Dick just enough but no more. He had also managed to issue a warning. Dick wondered how much more he knew, and had not told.

He crossed Silver Street and made his way along the Backs. King's College Chapel was romantically veiled in the early evening mist, with frost on the lawns sloping down to the river – a perfect tourist picture postcard. He entered St John's College by the rear gate, crossed the Pepys Bridge and made his way to the guest rooms in Chapel Court.

One of the privileges of membership of a Cambridge college was the right to a few nights free accommodation every year in the college guest rooms. Dick had never used this privilege before but he was glad of it now. He had not told Sally of his visit to Cambridge, and had no wish to meet her. It would only have led to disagreements over the divorce settlement. It was better to let the lawyers sort it all out.

He took a shower, then relaxed in the battered but comfortable armchair in his room. He felt that he needed to think things through, to somehow organise what he had discovered so far, so that he could make sense of it.

He knew for sure now that Vish and Molly had had some sort of special relationship with Keith Lennox in Delhi. The three of them had plotted to get rid of Dick, and then Nagarajan. Earlier, Dick had found out about Vish's crooked schemes and tried to have him dismissed. He had failed because Lennox had forbidden him to act against Vish. Why? Dick had only survived for a few months longer in the Madras factory, and he had been harassed with poison-pen letters and the death threat. But it was only when he had begun investigating the big Hosur factory contract that he had been sent on early retirement. What was the connection? And where did Molly's son John fit in? Who was his father? Was this the key to the whole affair?

Dick determined to speak to his old tutor, Sir Jeremy Jackson, the retired Professor of Comparative Philology. Jacko, as he was affectionately known by everyone in the college, was a famous eccentric. Some people even considered him to be mad. But he had been a Fellow of the College for over forty years and was a part of the place. And he knew the undergraduates personally. Unlike many professors, he spent a lot of time just chatting to students. He would certainly remember John Verghese. Dick called the Steward's office and booked himself for dinner at High

Table[31] the next day. Jacko was bound to be there; he never missed his three free meals a day.

Dick had eaten too much for lunch. He did not feel like going out into the cold night and sitting alone in some anonymous restaurant. He read for a while, then went to bed. It was only nine thirty. As he turned out the light, the thought of Lakshmi flashed through his mind. He wondered how she was coping with her father. Though it was ridiculous – he had met her only once – he found himself missing her. He told himself not to be a fool, and went to sleep.

*   *   *

He woke at six in the morning. The courtyard below was dark but filled with thick, milky fog. The windows were covered with patterns of frost. Distant footsteps echoed strangely on the cobblestones in the courtyard. He wrapped himself tighter in the bedclothes and slept again until seven.

He spent a lazy day. After breakfast in the college buttery, he strolled off into the town. He browsed in the bookshops, and bought a couple of collections of short stories for Lakshmi. He lunched at the Riverside Restaurant, overlooking the fateful place where he had fallen into the river. He wondered if his keys were still buried somewhere in the sticky, black mud.

In the afternoon he went to a film at the Arts Cinema, one of the places he used to go as a student. It was called "Wolf" and starred Jack Nicholson as a man who turns into a werewolf. It was oddly disturbing and he looked around at the audience in the cinema almost expecting to see human wolves.

After dressing for dinner, he walked across to the Senior Common Room for sherry. A handful of professors and guests were already there. He helped himself to a glass of college sherry and went to check the list of those dining that evening. Sure enough, Jacko's name was there. He recognised very few of the other names, except the Master's. He noted that a Nobel prize-winner and a well-known woman novelist were among the guests.

Jacko came in and walked straight across to him. He was a small, sprightly man, with a round stomach and twinkling eyes. His bald head was sun-tanned; he took a Mediterranean holiday every winter.

'Got your note, Dick. Splendid to see you again. Let me just get myself a drink. Right. Cheers. Just got back from my holiday in Greece. Lovely weather. Good to catch up with the latest Greek idiomatic expressions. I love it. How are you keeping?'

At a signal from the Master, everyone followed him in single file into the great hall and took their seats at the High Table on a raised platform at one end. Below them, the undergraduate students sat at the long tables under the portraits of famous former students, hanging on the wood-panelled walls. Everyone rose for grace[32] to be said, in Latin, of course.

Dick sat next to Jacko who, between mouthfuls of food, made rude comments in a loud voice about the other dinner guests. Jacko continued to do this for the entire meal. They then stood again for grace, again in Latin, and filed out.

'Come back to my rooms, Dick. I can't stand any more of this ridiculous talk. Can't hear myself think. We'll have some coffee sent over, and you can try my Slivovica. I got a bottle off one of my ex-students before the Bosnian thing started. Terrible business.'

Jacko's rooms were on the first floor facing the chapel. Although he must have been over eighty years old, he was clearly still active. A grammar of Albanian lay on the desk, next to a work on the phonology of Old Basque. Journals on linguistics were scattered around the room, and a large Mandarin–English dictionary with well-thumbed pages lay open on the dining table.

A college butler brought them a tray of coffee. Jacko uncorked a bottle of clear spirits, pungent with the aroma of plums.

'Here you are. This will put hair on your chest!' and he poured Dick a glass of the fiery liquid.

'Now, what can I do for you, Dick? What's your problem?'

Dick explained that he had some friends in India who were anxious to contact a student who had been at St John's until recently. It was not quite the truth but it was not a complete lie either. Jacko remembered the name immediately.

'John Verghese? Of course I know who you mean. A very nice chap. Anglo-Indian. Very intelligent. He got a first class degree in Economics last year. I have to admit that he was a bit of a disappointment to me though. I'd been hoping to use him as an informant on Malayalam; very interesting language, Malayalam, spoken in Kerala you know. Fascinating place. I went there many years ago when I was learning the language myself. Tamil, Telugu, Kannada and Malayalam: wonderful languages you know.

All as ancient as they come. Pushed down to the tip of the sub-continent by those terrible Aryans. I'd been hoping he could help me with translations I'd been doing of some ancient texts. Not a bit of it! The fellow didn't speak a word of his mother's language! In fact the poor chap had never set foot in India. Completely English. Terrible thing. Mind you, it happens all the time now. I get Arab students who can't read classical Arabic, Chinese students who can't write proper characters, only these miserable simplified things old Mao brought in, and Indian students who don't know a thing about Sanskrit. I don't know what the world's coming to.'

'Do you happen to know what happened to him after he went down from the University?'

'He went into a bank in London I think. We can easily check up on it tomorrow morning. Old Briggs was his tutor. Not a bad fellow, Briggs. He has a weakness for his colleagues' wives, but nobody's perfect. He's a good scholar in his way. He'll have Verghese's address, I've no doubt. I can't disturb him this evening though; he has a regular lady visitor on Thursdays I believe.'

Next morning he called on Jacko again after breakfast. He learned that John Verghese had taken up a job as a trainee at a well-known bank in the City.[33] Jacko handed him the address and a contact telephone number.

'There. Do give the boy my best regards if you look him up. Oh, and by the way, if you happen to be in Mysore next time you go to India, do look up old Aranganayagam at the Institute of Indian Languages. He's a wonderful old rogue. Terrible womaniser. You'd enjoy him. Tell him he still owes me that article. He'll know which one I mean.'

Dick took an afternoon train to London. The train broke down at Stevenage, and finally crawled into Kings Cross an hour and a half late. It was now the rush hour. To avoid the crowds, Dick had an early dinner at a Greek restaurant in Victoria. He got back to Hove at ten in the evening. There was a pile of junk mail in his mailbox, and one letter from his solicitor setting out details of the proposed divorce settlement. He put it to one side, and went straight to bed.

Chapter 10   *A Visit to Ned in Bath*

Dick spent the weekend thinking about the information he had gathered so far. He had to find out who John's real father was. That was obviously one of the keys to the conspiracy between Molly, Vish and Lennox. Sir Percy had told him that Molly's lover had been British. He needed to know which British staff had been in Madras in 1970. He remembered that Nagarajan had mentioned Ned Outram. Dick had never met Outram in person but he had heard plenty of stories about his sensational love life. He needed to check with Nagarajan. But he also needed to find out if there had been any other British staff in the factory at the time. One of them, he felt sure, had fathered Molly's child.

Just after lunch on Sunday he made an international call to Nagarajan. It would be about six in the evening in Devanahalli he calculated. It was Lakshmi who answered the phone. Dick realised immediately that he had been hoping that she would. Yet the moment he heard her voice, he felt a rising sense of unease, coupled with nervous excitement. He could not say what he really wanted to say to her.

'Hello? . . . Oh, Dick. You want to speak to my father I think?'

'Yes, I do – but I am so happy to speak to you too.'

'I am sorry but he is out with some friends. Can I take a

message for him? He will be back late tonight. Will you call again?'

'Lakshmi. I will call again. Did you hear what I said? I said I am so happy to speak to you. And I meant it.'

'Dick ... I am happy to hear your voice also. Very happy ...'

'Lakshmi. I got you a couple of books in England. I'll send them on tomorrow.'

'That's so lovely, Dick. I only wish I ... ' the line was suddenly cut. There was just a long whistling sound. Dick sat thinking for a long time. Just to hear Lakshmi's voice again had turned his emotions upside down.

An hour later he called Ramu at home in Madras. Ramu confirmed that Ned Outram had been in Madras at the time. More importantly, Ned and Keith Lennox had been the only British staff in the factory. That was what Dick needed to know. Molly's lover had been one of them.

He sat for a long time, wondering whether he should call Nagarajan's number again. He no longer needed information but he longed to hear Lakshmi's voice again. Finally he decided it was better not to call.

Instead he called Ramu again to get Outram's address. Ramu agreed to call him the following day, after checking the personnel records in the office.

*   *   *

At lunchtime the following day, Ramu rang through with the information. Ned was living in Bath. Ramu gave the address and telephone number. He also warned Dick to be careful. Vish had been asking questions in the factory about Dick's last visit.

'He is furious. You have touched a raw nerve – no doubt

about it,' said Ramu, with delight. 'Molly also has been asking all sorts of questions about your doings. I shall keep ears and eyes open, as usual.'

Dick called the Bath number several times before he managed to reach Ned. He sounded a bit vague, not quite connected to the real world. Eventually he agreed to see Dick the following day. He gave him directions on how to find the house. 'But don't expect too much my old friend,' he mumbled, 'I live in elegant poverty. You'll see. I do look forward to seeing you. I'm sure we'll find lots to talk about.'

*   *   *

Dick checked into a small hotel on the Weston Road in Bath. He had chosen it from the town street plan because it was within walking distance of Ned's house. Here he was above the town, with Audley Park sloping down towards the back of Royal Terrace. The houses were built from the golden yellow Bath stone, most of them eighteenth or nineteenth century – big houses standing in spacious gardens.

He found Ned's house in a narrow lane off the main road. It was a large, square, Victorian house standing in an untidy, overgrown garden, with a dark cypress tree in front of it.

Dick rang the doorbell, which echoed away deep inside the house. No one answered. Dick looked at his watch. It was six in the evening. He had told Ned to expect him between half past five and six. He rang again.

He was taken by surprise when a voice behind him said, 'It's no good ringing the door bell. You must be Dick Sterling. I forgot to mention that I don't live in the house.

Can't afford to. I let the house to some business people. I live in the servants' flat in the basement. Come on. I'll show you the way.'

He led the way down a narrow flight of steps to a small door in the stone wall. It opened into an airless room, full of dark furniture, and smelling of unwashed clothes, cooking oil and stale tobacco. In one corner there was a sink and a draining board full of dirty dishes. Ashtrays were scattered about, full of cigarette ends. Through an open doorway, Dick could see an unmade bed, clothes thrown on the floor. The overall effect was one of total neglect.

Dick turned his attention to his host. Ned Outram was about his own age. He must have been strikingly handsome once but now he was balding, and great grey bags hung down below his watery eyes. He wore dirty jeans and a grey denim shirt under a dirty white woollen sweater. His belly hung out over the waist of his jeans, from years of beer drinking.

'Sorry about the mess,' he said, though it was not a real apology. 'I've got used to living on my own, and I've forgotten how "normal" people live – that is, if I ever knew. Shall I make you some coffee or tea? Or can I offer you something a bit more exciting? Vodka? Tequila? You say, and I'll tell you whether I've got it.'

Dick saw the empty bottles by the sink, which explained the unreality in which Ned seemed to be living.

'No thanks, Ned. I don't need anything for the moment. I just wanted to ask you a few questions about the time you were in Madras with the company.'

'Oh yes, the company. The wonderful company. The company that will take care of us all for all time. The jolly old company that will do anything to survive. Forget the company! It was the company that ruined my life. So don't talk to me about the company.'

'I think I know how you feel. After all, something similar happened to me. Do you feel like telling me about it? I mean about what they did to you?'

'Well, they kicked me out, if that's what you mean. It was in 1980. I'd been there for ten years by then. They invented something and got rid of me.'

'But who were "they"?' Dick asked.

'The bloody Visvanathans! God knows how they did it, but they did. It was as if the top management were blind. They only listened to what the Visvanathans told them.'

'But I thought you got along pretty well – with Molly especially.'

'What do you mean by that exactly?' asked Ned, his face suddenly red with anger.

'Well, the way I heard it, you and Molly had quite a thing going back in 1970. And there were a lot of rumours about Molly going on special leave to the UK for a year.'

'You must be joking!' said Ned. 'Molly was an absolute bitch. Do you understand what I mean by that? She would have done any*thing* with any*one* to get ahead. She was totally available, at a price. It wasn't a price I wanted to pay. Yes, we did go out once or twice. Yes, she did stay back at my place once – but only once. I don't make a habit of sleeping with snakes.'

'So who was the father of Molly's child, then?' Dick asked directly.

'Look, I don't want to accuse anyone, but I know Barbara Lennox wasn't around for a couple of months. And

I know that Lennox wasn't as pure as he pretended to be. And I know that Molly did go to his place at least once – and stayed there. You know what the gossip is like in Madras. You can check it with Ramu if you don't believe me. And I'm damned sure that I didn't give her a child.'

'What makes you so sure?'

'Well, believe it or not, I'm not capable of giving anyone a baby. I had myself tested way back when my marriage was breaking up. There's no way that child could have been mine. I'm infertile. I couldn't give a baby to anyone.'

Chapter 11 *London: John Verghese*

They met at the small Italian restaurant, La Perla, in Greek Street, Soho. Dick had contacted John Verghese at Barings Bank a few days previously. He had arranged the lunch by claiming to be the close friend of Keith Lennox, and by mentioning Jacko.

John was tall and athletic in a truly striking way. He moved with the grace and confidence of a wild animal, yet his smile was kind. He seemed like a really nice human being. Dick noted from his light-brown skin colour that there was no doubt of his Anglo-Indian parentage.

Over the 'antipasto' Dick tried to find out just how much John knew about his own origins.

'Well, I've been so incredibly lucky,' he said. 'After my parents were killed, Keith and Barbara were really wonderful. In fact, I don't remember my real parents at all. I was too young. It was Keith and Barbara who felt like my real parents. I think I spent every holiday with them or with their family. Jane – you know Jane, their daughter – well Jane and I were even thinking of getting married at one point – but Uncle Keith stepped in and stopped it. Maybe it's best – and my uncle and auntie in India were also incredibly kind and helpful.'

'Your uncle and auntie?' Dick queried.

'Yes. I'm sure you must have run into them in Madras.

Auntie Molly and Uncle Vish. They always visit me whenever they come over to the UK.'

Dick felt that the pieces of the puzzle were beginning to fall into place. By the time the meal was over, Dick was sure that he knew what lay behind the twenty-year-old story.

*   *   *

Dick spent the next month collecting documents as evidence. He obtained a copy of John's birth certificate from St Catherine's House in the Strand. He traced the private hospital where John had been born and got copies of the receipts, paid for by Lennox. He confirmed that John had attended a well-known Catholic public school – and obtained copies of the school bills, also paid by Keith Lennox.

He obtained, through Ramu, some interesting records concerning the Hosur factory project. The company had originally been offered the land at a special, cheap price but this offer had 'disappeared'. Instead, the company had paid forty per cent more for the land for their new factory. Vish and Molly had collected twenty per cent of the difference from the sellers. And Lennox had known of this and done nothing. Ramu's documents included a copy of the original offer!

He also heard from Ned again, sending him a yellowing photograph of Lennox and Molly. They were standing close, looking into each other's eyes. He had his arm around her. It was a picture of young lovers. How Ned had got hold of it he had no idea – but it was just one more small piece of the jigsaw puzzle.

Slowly and carefully, Dick built up a file proving extensive corruption by the Visvanathans under the protection of Keith Lennox. The only possible motives for Lennox's action were either financial gain for himself or to hide the scandal of Molly and the illegitimate child. (Dick recalled the public disgrace which Keith would have experienced if his relationship had become known. Things have changed now, but at the time, mixed-race affairs were highly disapproved of by both Europeans and Indians.) In either case, he would have been in deep trouble if it had ever been made public. Dick felt a rising sense of anger. Revenge would be sweet!

Ramu had hinted in his letter that Nagarajan knew even more. It was not difficult for Dick to make up his mind to return to India. The thought of Lakshmi alone was enough.

Chapter 12   *Nandi Hills*

Dick spent only one night at the club in Madras before flying on to Bangalore. But, soon after going to bed, he was disturbed by two telephone calls.

One was from Ramu. He had heard that the Visvanathans were planning something. He did not know what it was, but it had to do with Dick's inquiries. Dick had obviously touched a raw nerve. Ramu advised him to be very careful. 'These guys are dangerous. They will stop at nothing to save themselves. Be very careful Dick. I will go on looking around and contact you as necessary. You will be at West End or Nagarajan's?' Dick told him to try either.

The other call was anonymous. When Dick picked up the phone a muffled voice simply said, 'You'd better get back to the UK where you belong. Remember your death threat? This time we're not playing games. Mind your own business – or else . . .'

He spent an uncomfortable night, tossing and turning in a half-sleep, before the dawn birdsong finally woke him.

*   *   *

The West End was, as always, a welcome oasis in the clouds of traffic pollution of Bangalore. Dick made a call to Devanahalli. The number did not answer. He decided to hire a car anyway and to leave early the next morning.

The driver turned out to be Shaukat, the same man who

had driven him on the previous occasion. By half past seven they were again in the thick of the morning traffic, and by nine they were in Devanahalli. Neither Dick nor Shaukat had noticed the black Ambassador with dark windows which had left the West End just after them, and followed them at a safe distance all the way to Devanahalli.

As Shaukat drove the car into the dusty lane, Dick felt butterflies in his stomach. Would Lakshmi be there? What would he say to her? What would her reaction be? Did she have the same feelings for him as he had for her? After all, they had only spoken a few words on the phone. He was basing everything on the glances they had exchanged the last time, on the half-spoken hints on the telephone, on his own feelings. Perhaps he was imagining it all. Why should anyone as beautiful as Lakshmi be in the least interested in a man almost twice her age, with his career in ruins behind him, and from a completely different culture? He cursed himself for building up so many hopes on so little evidence. Yet his hands were trembling as he knocked on the street door.

It was Lakshmi herself who opened the door. She was plainly taken completely by surprise. Her face showed shock, then joy, then worry, almost pain. Then she smiled the most wonderful smile and asked him to come in. He followed her across the courtyard to the living quarters. She was wearing a simple cotton sari of a deep turquoise colour, with a thin border of crimson and gold. She moved with all the grace he remembered.

As she prepared coffee, they talked. It felt as if they had always known each other. Her tense nervousness had left her. She was warm and relaxed. Could this be because her father was not there? Dick wondered.

'I tried to call you from Bangalore yesterday,' he said, 'but then I decided to come anyway.'

'I'm so glad you did, Dick; our phone's out of order as usual, but my father is away I'm afraid. He has gone to the wedding of a nephew in Anantapur. But he is due back this evening. I hope you can stay to see him. I can make you some lunch later. He should be back by nightfall. He will be very upset if he finds out he has missed you.'

'Of course I'll stay but I don't want to put you to any trouble. I mean . . .'

'It's no trouble at all. Quite the opposite.' She paused, as if in doubt about what she was going to say. When she spoke, her voice was darker, more serious, 'Dick, I'm sorry but I lied to you last time.'

'What do you mean, "lied"?'

'I told you I was not lonely here. In fact I'm desperately lonely. It is so isolated here. I have no-one I can talk to – really talk to. There is nowhere to go. Nothing to do except to take care of my father. And he is becoming more and more difficult. You saw for yourself last time. So I would be so happy if you would stay until he comes back. I would like to know you better. Will you stay?'

'Of course I'll stay. Maybe I shouldn't say this, but . . . I didn't come here again just to see your father. I have thought of you often since I left. I came to see you too.'

Lakshmi looked down. He wondered if he had said too much, too soon. But when she looked up, she had a radiant smile of pure joy on her face. She said nothing but poured his coffee for him. Her eyes did not leave his face for a moment as he drank it.

'I know what,' said Dick suddenly. 'Why don't we go out for the day? I've got the car and the driver. There must be somewhere interesting we could go. And it would make a change for you, wouldn't it?'

'That's a lovely idea Dick. But aren't you tired? I don't mind preparing lunch . . .'

'No. Come on Lakshmi. Let's enjoy ourselves. Where's the nearest place we could go?'

'Well, there's Nandi Hills, which isn't far away. It would only take about half an hour or so to get to. It was one of Tipoo's[34] forts. Then the British made it into a sort of small hill station[35] for holidays in the hot season. There are some nice walks at the top.'

'Is there anywhere we can get lunch there?'

'I think there are a couple of small places, if you don't mind the Indian food.'

'Great. That's settled then. I'll wait while you get ready and then we'll go.'

Lakshmi returned fifteen minutes later wearing jeans and a shirt. She had tied her hair up in a bun. She looked younger, more athletic.

'I hope you don't mind,' she said, 'I can't go climbing about up there in a sari.'

As they drove out of the lane, the black Ambassador slid out from behind a parked lorry and followed them. Dick and Lakshmi were both too absorbed in their conversation to notice it but Shaukat frowned as he looked in the rear mirror. He had seen the car behind them in the morning. It seemed odd that it should be behind them again now. But he said nothing.

Dick wanted to see some statues he had read about in a

temple not far from Devanahalli, so they stopped on the way to the hills.

They parked the car in the small dusty lane leading up to the temple entrance. There were the usual small shops selling garlands of jasmine flowers, coconuts and bananas as offerings to the gods, cigarettes and soft drinks, and a variety of cheap-looking copies of the temple statues. Monkeys were fighting over scraps of food in the shade of a big raintree below the temple steps.

From the outside the temple was unimpressive; large granite blocks with very little decoration. But inside it was fantastic. The heavy stone roof was supported by hundreds of pillars, each one carved in the shape of gods, temple dancers, cows, lions, and other, mythical animals. The variety was almost too much, yet somehow it all seemed to fit together. Dick went from pillar to pillar trying to absorb the wealth of detail in each figure.

Lakshmi found him standing absorbed in front of a statue of a temple dancer. The naked figure was caught in mid-movement, gracefully standing on one leg, the other raised to knee-height. One arm was held slightly away from the body, the hand hanging loosely down. The other arm was held at shoulder height, the fingers formed into a graceful 'mudra'.[36] The breasts were full and naked, the angle of the hips and thighs voluptuously erotic, yet not in the least vulgar. The face shone with a kind of peaceful delight. Dick thought of Lakshmi's smile earlier.

'Now, I wonder what you're thinking?' Lakshmi said from behind him. He turned with a guilty look on his face, hoping she could not see into his thoughts. 'What are you blushing for?'

A Brahmin priest appeared and offered to chant prayers for them. He did so, then broke a coconut as an offering. Finally they both took 'aarti',[37] touching their fingers to the burning camphor and taking a spoonful of Ganga water in the palms of their hands before drinking it.

As they left the temple, Dick felt that the ceremony they had just performed had tied them still closer together in a way he could not define. They were both silent as they walked back to the car.

As the car turned out on to the main road again, the parked black Ambassador once again followed. Shaukat recognised the car and he speeded up. The other car speeded up too.

The narrow road to the top of Nandi Hills winds up in a series of over thirty tight hairpin bends to a point over 1500 metres above sea-level. The hills are covered by thorn bushes and eucalyptus trees but there is a lot of bare granite rock exposed to the burning dry heat.

As they negotiated each bend, Shaukat had to change down into first gear, and the car shook as it staggered up the next straight slope. With every bend, the view extended until they could see far away across the brown, dusty plateau to other groups of hills in the far distance. Eventually they passed through the narrow gateway into the fort and drove up to the summit.

There were a few groups of noisy schoolchildren being looked after by tired-looking teachers, and two or three families out for the day. Otherwise there was hardly anyone. There were a few restaurants. Lakshmi decided that the least bad would probably be the one run by the State Tourism Authority. It had the advantage of being perched on the edge of the mountain top, overlooking the precipice.

They took their seats at a dirty table next to the window, which gave a magnificent view of the surrounding landscape. Soon after they had ordered from the menu, a group of three men came in and sat at a table on the other side of the room. Two of them were very dark-skinned and looked thin and hungry. They were dressed in lunghis[38] and white shirts which had not been washed for a long time. The third one was pale and fat, with a thick black moustache. He was wearing spotlessly clean white trousers and shirt, with the collar turned up, and a pair of black and white shoes. He reminded Dick of a famous Tamil film star. He was obviously the leader and ordered beer and snacks for the group. They were soon in deep conversation. Dick did not like the look of them, nor the way they kept glancing over in his and Lakshmi's direction. He felt sure they were talking about them.

But soon Dick and Lakshmi were so deeply absorbed in each other that they forgot all about the men at the other table. They talked mainly about themselves. Dick told her about his forced retirement, about the break-up of his marriage, about his present inquiry and his hopes of revenge. A shadow passed across her face when he spoke of revenge – but he did not notice it at the time.

Lakshmi listened silently. Then she began to tell him about her own marriage; the way she had been 'advertised' in the 'brides' column[39] of the newspaper, then 'inspected' by the boy's family; how the dowry[40] had been agreed, and how, finally, she had married Girijan and moved to Udipi to live with his family. The Indian mother-in-law is not always as cruel as so often described but clearly Lakshmi had been unlucky. She was badly treated and made to work harder than a servant. And Girijan had been a weak man; certainly not able to stand up to his forceful mother. Things had been worse because Lakshmi had had no children. She had been made to feel guilty by all those malicious relatives and their questions, 'Any good news?', and their meaningful looks when she had had to answer, 'Not yet'.

'But Dick, I couldn't do it all on my own . . .'

Dick was about to ask the obvious question when he noticed the great wall of black cloud building up on the horizon and the flashes of lightning.

'The monsoon is due anytime,' said Lakshmi. 'I hope it won't break tonight.'

So Dick's questions went unanswered and they talked instead about Tipoo Sultan, who had built the fort, and who had ruled a large kingdom in southern India until defeated by the British at Srirangapatnam, just outside Mysore. Tiger Tipoo had been a forceful leader and a man without pity. Just below the restaurant where they now sat was Tipoo's Drop, a vertical rock face which fell 350 metres to the rocks below. One of Tipoo's famous punishments was to have his enemies thrown over the edge on to the rocks below.

'Let's go and see it before we leave,' Dick suggested.

'All right. But let's hurry; it's already three o'clock.'

Dick realised with a start that they had been talking for over two hours. As they got up to leave, he noticed that the men at the other table had gone. He felt vaguely relieved.

Outside a hot wind had started to blow. They walked

down past a small crumbling temple and a few low buildings, out on to the bare top of the mountain. The granite was flaking in layers, like the scalp of some ancient giant. Dick recalled that these were the most ancient rocks on earth. Almost nothing grew there, only some dry grass clinging to cracks in the rocks. As they moved down the skull of the mountain, he looked back at the ominous silhouette of the temple on the brow of the slope.

Eventually they reached the place where people said Tipoo had got rid of his enemies. There was a crumbling brick wall, overgrown by plants. In the wall there was a gap. Dick moved forward and looked over the edge. There was a vertical drop to the plain below. He pulled himself back nervously. He had an instinctive fear of heights.

Lakshmi excused herself for a few minutes – 'Nature calls,' she said – and walked off into some bushes further up the slope. Leaning on the wall Dick looked out over the plain to where lightning now flashed along the horizon and the black clouds looked like mountains behind it. He heard a footstep and turned, assuming it was Lakshmi.

As he turned, two of the men from the restaurant threw themselves at him. Each one grabbed an arm and began to force him backwards towards the gap in the wall. He could feel the rough bricks digging into his back. The leader, the man with the black and white shoes, stood a few yards back shouting to them in Tamil. Dick struggled hard and managed to free one arm and push the first man backwards. Then he swung the second man hanging on to his other arm in a wide circle until his head hit the wall with a dull thud. The leader and the first man both ran at him together. The leader had taken out a knife – but he never had time to use it. Lakshmi came racing down the slope giving out a terrifying scream and, with a classic karate kick to the man's wrist, sent the knife flying high into the air and over the wall. Dick managed to punch the side of the first man's head. Both men now turned away and half ran, half staggered down into the trees. Dick looked round for the second man but he was gone. Then there was the sound of a car driving off at speed.

Dick sat down and leaned his back against the wall. He was shaking and his face was white from the shock. Lakshmi knelt by him.

'Dick? There's blood on your shirt. Let me look.'

'It's OK I think. Just a few scratches on my arms. And my back feels sore. I think I must have bruised it on the wall. Nothing serious. Lakshmi, I think you saved my life just now. But where did you learn to kick like that?'

'I was in the karate team when I was at university, Dick. I always knew it would come in useful one day. But we must get away from here. They may try to attack us again. Can you walk all right?'

Dick got shakily to his feet and they made their way back to the car park, taking care to stay in the open. Shaukat noticed the blood on Dick's shirt but he said nothing until they were halfway down the hill.

'There was one black Ambassador following us always today, sir. It has gone. There were three goondas[41] who drove off fast as hell itself. I hope all is well sir?'

They kept a careful watch all the way back to Devanahalli but there was no sign of the black Ambassador. The goondas had obviously decided they had had enough for one day.

Chapter 13   *Devanahalli, May 1990*

After Dick had taken a hot bath, Lakshmi rubbed a sweet-smelling ointment into the deep scratches on his arm and along his back. She gave him one of her father's white cotton kurta pyjama[42] outfits to wear while she washed his shirt for him. He was beginning to feel less tense.

'But why do you think they attacked you, Dick? Does it have anything to do with what you told me at lunchtime? Why would anyone try to kill you? Because I'm sure that's what they were trying to do.'

'And they might have succeeded if it hadn't been for you, Lakshmi. I don't know how to thank you. They must have been trailing us all day, just waiting for the right opportunity. It frightens me to think about it. Anyway, I'm sure you're right – it must be connected to the inquiries I've been making. Someone obviously wants to stop me very badly.'

'Dick, don't you think you should give up this scheme of yours? What good can it do you? It is not good to become obsessed by revenge.'

'I can't stop now. I've got almost all the information I need. Why should they get away with all the terrible things they've been doing for so many years? Do you realise how much suffering they've caused other people, and I don't just mean me – look at your own father ... No, I can't stop now. All I need to do is to decide how I'm going to use the information I've got so as to cause them the most trouble.'

There was a long pause. Lakshmi looked worried and upset. Eventually she broke the awkward silence.

'I don't think it is right to take revenge. People are punished for their actions by what they become. God arranges punishment. We should leave it to him.'

'But that's just fatalism,' said Dick, 'and it means that criminals all over the place get away with the most dreadful crimes against other people.'

'Please think about what I have said,' said Lakshmi, 'if only because I believe you are now in great danger. And ... and ... I am afraid of what they might do to you.'

She left the room in tears and did not return for over an hour. Dick sat alone with his thoughts.

It was six by the time she came back. Dick had decided what he had to do. He rose to leave.

'I must go back to Bangalore, Lakshmi. Tomorrow I'll fly to Madras. I need to speak to the Visvanathans face-to-face. I should have done it before. Then at least they'll know what they're up against.'

'But Dick, that's walking into trouble. Please don't do it.'

'Don't worry, Lakshmi. I've had an idea. It will be my life insurance policy. I'll tell you about it in a minute.'

'But you can't leave now anyway. My father should be back any time. And it's getting dark. It isn't safe for you to travel in the dark. Supposing those men are waiting for you. Please don't leave. I'm sorry if I upset you by what I said. I meant it but I can understand how you feel too. Just don't leave me now. We've had such a lovely day together – well, most of it was lovely, I mean before they tried to kill you! Who knows when we may be able to see each other again? Please Dick.'

'OK, I'll wait until your father comes back, then I'll decide whether to stay on till tomorrow or not,' Dick said.

Lakshmi began to prepare supper. Dick sat watching her. But somehow the easy familiarity they had felt earlier in the day had evaporated. They felt awkward and did not know quite what to say to each other. Perhaps it was their disagreement. Perhaps it was the thought that Nagarajan might walk in at any moment. Perhaps it was the realisation that they might never meet again. In the distance there was the sound of thunder. The air was hot and suffocating.

By seven thirty, Nagarajan had still not returned. They ate supper. Lakshmi looked nervous and worried.

'Are you worried about your father?'

'No. I'm sure he's all right. If he isn't back by eight, there's not much point in waiting for him. It isn't the first time he has stayed longer than expected. He probably found some old friends to drink with and talk about "the good old days". He'll come back when he's ready.'

Eight o'clock came and went. Dick did not know what to do. He knew he should leave but he did not want to. Lakshmi had become very important to him but somehow things had gone wrong between them. And now he felt unsure of what to do about it. Eventually he took his courage in both hands and spoke.

'Lakshmi. I don't want to lose you. I'm sorry about our disagreement. I don't want to go back to Bangalore this evening but I don't know if I should stay. Won't it be bad for your reputation? What about your neighbours? Won't they talk? Tell me what you want me to do.'

Lakshmi looked him full in the eyes, then walked across to where he was sitting. She took both his hands in hers and held them.

'I don't care about my reputation, or about what the neighbours might say. I've had enough of this life. It isn't a real life at all. Please stay, Dick. Who knows, my father may turn up after all. Tell your driver to find a place to stay till the morning, then come back and we'll talk.'

They went on talking till midnight. The electricity had gone off soon after nine, probably because of the storm which they could still hear in the distance. So they sat talking by candlelight. The sense of easy familiarity had returned between them.

Dick gave Lakshmi the sealed packet he had brought with him. In it was a copy of all the documents he had collected about the Visvanathans and Lennox. If anything happened to him, she was to send it by registered post to London, to the chairman of the board of directors of Trakton, and to the *Daily Mail* newspaper.

Eventually Dick got up and they made their way across the courtyard – Dick to his room, Lakshmi to hers. Her father's room was between them. As they said goodnight, Dick took Lakshmi in his arms and began to kiss her gently, on her hair, her neck, her cheeks.

Just at that moment there was a sudden blinding flash of lightning. Thunder shook the the house and heavy rain began to pour down in torrents, soaking them both.

'Come inside,' Lakshmi said softly.

In her room she fell into his arms. He felt her body close

to him. He lifted her face to him and kissed her. They kissed long and deep, their bodies close against each other. He felt her soft mouth opening for him, her full breasts pressing urgently against him, her hands caressing him. He remembered the temple statue he had seen earlier in the day, and the image melted into the reality of Lakshmi in his arms. As they lay down together, nothing existed except this moment of total surrender to each other. It was as if they had become one person, fused together in this white hot moment of pleasure.

'I love you, Lakshmi.'

'I love you too, Dick,' she murmured. 'Hold me, Dick please. I need to feel you again.'

The storm outside grew quieter but the rain continued to pour until morning. They slept little, and between sleeping and loving, they had long whispered conversations.

*   *   *

Dick stayed with Lakshmi until after lunch. They were both happy to be with each other. He had never felt closer to anyone in his life. They agreed that they would meet as soon as Dick's business with Trakton was over. They made no definite plans but there was an unspoken understanding between them about a future life together.

Lakshmi again saw him off. The lane was full of pools of water from the night rain. She stood waving as the car turned out of the lane. Behind her, the Nandi Hills were sharply outlined against the rain-washed air.

Chapter 14 *Kidnap*

The car bumped over the rough holes on the Mahabalipuram road out of Madras. Dick sat in the back, uncomfortably squeezed between two men in dirty white shirts and lunghis. Their leader sat in the front seat with the driver and the other man, who had introduced himself as Satish.

'But this isn't the way to Kalakshetra Colony,' Dick protested as they passed the Marundheshwarar temple in Tiruvanmiyur. 'We've passed it already.'

'We are going somewhere quieter,' said Satish menacingly. 'Please do not be alarmed. And don't even think of trying anything.'

But the palms of Dick's hands began to sweat as they drove farther and farther out of the city. The two men in the back stank of stale cigarettes, coconut oil pomade and paan.[43] He began to feel sick. And he cursed himself for being so stupid.

* * *

As soon as he had returned to Madras, he had called Vish to arrange a meeting. Vish had been unusually polite, even friendly. He had agreed to come to Dick's room at the club at six the following evening. Instead, he had sent Satish with a message to say that he was unwell but could see Dick at home. The car would take him and bring him back. Dick had been deceived by Satish's educated accent and smart appearance. Satish had politely held the back door open for him outside the club. He himself had got in next to the driver. Everything seemed so normal and civilised.

But when the car reached the Theosophical Society[44] grounds it slowed down and stopped. The back doors on both sides were thrown open and two men jumped in, one on either side of him. Dick immediately recognised them as his attackers at Nandi Hills. At the same time, their leader got into the front seat beside Satish. Dick had struggled to get out of the car but one of the men pressed something hard and sharp into his side. By then the car was speeding out of the city, and the dark windows made it impossible for him to attract anyone's attention outside. He had fallen into the trap like an idiot.

The car bumped quickly along the narrow road in the dark. From time to time it slowed to avoid the water lorries, driving towards them at high speed in the middle of the road. Madras is permanently short of water, and water is driven into the city in lorries. But the drivers were often drunk on toddy or arrack[45] and drove with no thought for others, and usually without headlights!

Shortly after passing Cholamandel, the artists' village, the car turned off left towards the sea along a rough track. It stopped outside a large house overlooking the beach. Dick looked around. There were no other houses in sight.

*   *   *

The house was newly-built, and furnished with all the luxury Dick remembered from the Visvanathans' apartment in Kalakshetra all those years ago. They had

87

obviously got even richer. He was shown into a large room with a terrace overlooking the sea.

He was left there with the leader guarding the door. It was half an hour before Vish and Molly came into the room. By then he was feeling distinctly nervous.

Vish had put on weight. He waddled heavily into the room. His eyes, mouth and nose were now surrounded by fat. It was as if a small, clever rat sat trapped in the middle of a labyrinth of fleshy folds. His eyes were as sharp and snake-like as ever though, and his mouth wore the unpleasant smile Dick remembered so well, revealing his two large front teeth. Molly too had put on weight, but she dressed to conceal it. The rich Mysore silk sari was carefully folded around her, but even that could not hide the fat backflaps of flesh bulging out between her choli[46] and her waist. She wore more make-up than Dick remembered. But her eyes too shone dangerously, just as they had when he saw her last. If Vish was the rat, she was the snake.

'So, we meet again. Only this time you're not any more the boss. In fact, you were never the boss, as you know now. It seems you have been interfering in things which don't concern you.'

'Don't concern me?' said Dick. 'I seem to remember I lost my job because of them. And so did some of my friends.'

'That's just your imagination. Who will believe you? You're just trying to find someone to blame.'

'You're so pathetic,' Molly added, in her high-pitched, nasal voice. 'I suppose you know that none of the staff ever respected you. I can't say I blame them.' She flashed a look of pure hatred at him. Dick kept silent, refusing to respond. He wanted to know where all this was leading before he said anything.

Vish spoke again. 'Anyway, even if you tell what you say you know, what difference will it make to us? Who cares about these things? We'll just deny it all anyway. And you can't touch us here. You're just an interfering foreigner. And I've got plenty of friends who can take care of you.'

Dick decided that the time had come to speak. 'Oh, I think quite a lot of people would be interested, don't you? There's John Verghese for a start. I'm sure he'd be pleased to find out who his real parents are. He'd be delighted to know that his mother abandoned him as a baby.'

'You bastard!' Molly screamed. 'Do you think I'd let you get away with that?'

Dick suddenly realised that he had won. They did not know he had found out about Molly's child. They only knew about his inquiries into the Hosur factory affair. He had got them in a corner.

'And I'm sure that Barbara Lennox would be delighted to find out that her husband has been deceiving her for over twenty years,' Dick went on, ignoring Molly's explosion of anger. 'And, don't you think that the board of directors at Trakton would be interested to find out that you two have stolen enormous sums of company money? And that Lennox knew all about it and did nothing? And I doubt whether even your "friends" would be able to stop a nice juicy story about it in *India Today* or the *Hindu*. And I think Trakton has enough high-level contacts to make sure they'd win a case against you in the courts. After all, I calculate you made over two crores out of the Hosur land deal alone. I wonder how much of that went to your friend

Lennox? So, I reckon there would be quite a lot of people who would be interested. And you've made plenty of enemies over the years. Once you were down, there would be plenty of people ready to kick you. Think about it.'

'We have already thought about it,' said Vish, threateningly, 'and we've decided that we can't let you go around spreading your white man's dirt about us. You seem to forget that I am a Brahmin. Do you think I can allow a shit-face like you to pollute me? You must be out of your mind.'

'I don't see that you can do anything to stop me,' said Dick, but his heart was beginning to beat faster as he said so.

'Oh no?' Vish replied, 'I think it is quite simple to do something. Just step outside for a moment.'

They moved to the terrace. Dick could hear the wind in the palm trees. The waves pounded heavily on the beach below. It was cloudy and pitch dark. He could just make out the white foam capping the waves as they broke.

'It's a lovely night for a swim, isn't it?' said Vish, menacingly. 'Of course, the sea is very powerful here. People are always getting carried away. Especially foreign tourists who don't realise the danger. It's worse if they're drunk of course. And you will be drunk. Shankar – come!'

The man with the black and white shoes moved quickly behind Dick and held his arms. The other two men pushed him back into the room and tied him to a chair. Satish stood behind him and pulled his head back. They forced his mouth open and poured in a glass of whisky. He coughed and spluttered, but most of it went down.

'You always were a heavy drinker, weren't you?' came

Molly's voice from behind him. 'Such a pity you never learned when to stop . . . So decadent really.'

Dick knew that, if he didn't speak up now, he was finished. His body would be washed up somewhere down the coast and no-one would ever suspect murder.

'There's just one thing,' he shouted, as the men pulled his head back again. 'If anything happens to me, one set of the papers containing the evidence will be sent to Trakton. Another set will go to the newspapers. Accidents may happen – but they'd better not happen to me!'

The men suddenly let go of his head. He could not see what was happening but he overheard a confused, whispered discussion in Tamil going on behind him. After what seemed a very long time, Vish waddled round the chair to face him. He leaned towards him with an evil, angry look on his face.

'All right. You win – today. I'm going to let you go. But just remember, if you tell what you know, I will get you. Because, by then, I will have nothing more to lose. So, my dear "boss", get to hell out of here, and don't forget what I've told you.'

They took Dick out to the car and pushed him into it. Then they drove off, but not in the direction of Madras. A few kilometres down the road, the car slowed and Dick was pushed out onto the roadside. The car reversed and drove quickly back the way it had come.

*   *   *

Dick slept late the following morning. He had been picked up by a late night hotel tourist bus which had dropped him off in town at eleven in the night. He had taken an auto back to the club, feeling shaken but oddly confident. He tried to call Lakshmi but without success. Then he fell into a deep and dreamless sleep.

The following day, he called Ramu and arranged to have lunch with him. Luckily, British Airways had a seat on the next day's flight to London. He booked it. The rest of the morning he spent in his room, trying to reach Lakshmi. He did not succeed. He hurriedly scribbled her a note, telling her what had happened and reassuring her that he was OK.

In the club dining room, surrounded by white-uniformed waiters, his recent adventure seemed incredible. He told Ramu all about it, and about what he proposed to do next in London. Ramu was, as always, supportive. Dick asked him to continue to try to contact Lakshmi. It was as he was leaving that Ramu mentioned that he himself was considering early retirement.

'Not like you of course; mine will be voluntary,' he said with a smile. 'Only I feel I want to do something on my own. Maybe start my own company, something like that, now that the government economic policy is more liberal, encouraging foreign investment and all that. Why don't you join me? You've got lots of experience, plenty of contacts and you know the Indian scene. We would make highly suitable partners. Think about it.'

Chapter 15 *Teatime in Barnes: London, June 1990*

It was not difficult to arrange to meet Barbara Lennox. She remembered him, of course, and agreed to see him again to hear news of her good friends, the Visvanathans. Keith was away on a business trip to Thailand. She invited Dick to tea in Barnes on Saturday afternoon.

London was enjoying fine summer weather, so Dick decided to take the underground to Hammersmith, then walk across the bridge to Barnes. He passed pubs smelling of warm beer, full of afternoon customers. There was a feeling of relaxation in the air, with young couples strolling hand-in-hand, men with their shirts off mowing their lawns, red-legged women slumped in deckchairs in their front gardens, children playing half-naked in the park. It was Britain at its most casual, happy to forget, in this temporary sunshine, the miseries of unemployment and recession.

The Lennoxes had a large Victorian house overlooking the pond in Barnes. Barnes was the territory of the successful – business executives, bankers, computer whizz-kids, retired diplomats – all those who had made it, and kept it!

Barbara answered the door herself and led Dick into a large, sun-filled room which looked out directly onto the large garden behind the house. It was a comfortable room with large armchairs and tables covered with family photographs and souvenirs. Dick noticed a picture of John Verghese standing with Keith and Barbara at a school prize-giving. There were also pictures of the Lennox's daughter Jane, an attractive red-head.

Barbara had prepared a tray with tea and small home-made cakes. Dick recalled that she had always been proud of her home and her cooking skills. She poured the tea.

'So, how is everyone over there?' she asked, with a slight Scottish accent.

Dick spoke in general terms about the Visvanathans, about Ramu, about Nagarajan ... He was careful not to betray his feelings about any of them.

'Oh yes, Nagarajan. Such a nice man. I believe he took early retirement. Such a pity about his wife. I heard that his daughter had lost her husband too. So sad.'

Dick had a sharp feeling of loss as she said this. It was strange to hear Lakshmi referred to in the third person, like a stranger.

As the conversation went on, Dick gently tried to discover just how much Barbara knew about John Verghese, and about Keith's relationship with him. He decided that, unless she was a superb actress, she knew nothing. She talked about how they had taken care of him during school holidays.

'The poor child had lost both his parents in a car accident,' she explained. 'It was the least we could do. And somehow we felt we kept in touch with India through him. He became part of the family in a way. There was even a time when he and Jane were in love, at least they said they were. I would have liked them to get married. It sort of felt right in a way, if you know what I mean. But Keith was absolutely against it. I've never seen him so upset. I could never understand why. After all, he's not colour-prejudiced or anything like that. But there was no way I could talk him round. Funny really. Anyway, Jane married Nigel last year. He's a diplomat and they're in Senegal now. I'm afraid they're not very happy though. Still, you can't have everything in a marriage, can you?'

She sounded suddenly old and tired. It was as if a worrying thought had crossed her mind.

Then she smiled and went on to talk about Keith. He was now Chief Executive. He had even been contacted unofficially to find out whether he would accept a knighthood and become Sir Keith Lennox. She thought it would be lovely if he would.

'Then he could retire and we'd maybe see a bit more of each other.'

Dick left, feeling that Barbara was a nice, homely woman, who had no idea of the web of deceit which surrounded her. She would be totally shocked if she ever discovered the truth. He was glad to know that. It would be a weapon he could use in his meeting with Lennox.

Barbara kissed him on the cheek as he left. She smelt faintly of old lavender. It reminded him of his childhood. He almost regretted what he was about to do to her.

Chapter 16   *The showdown: London, June 1990*

It was not so easy to arrange a meeting with Lennox himself. Dick called the company headquarters several times. Each time he was told that Lennox was away. Finally, he called Barbara to find out when he would be back. She gave him a date a week later.

Meantime, he had been trying desperately to reach Lakshmi by phone. He even left messages with Ramu to try to contact her. He needed to speak to her urgently. In the end, he wrote her a long, carefully-worded letter. In it he told her that his divorce from Sally had finally come through. He asked her to marry him. When he had written it, Dick walked down towards the sea to post it. A light summer drizzle had started to fall, and the late afternoon holiday-makers were packing up their things and leaving the beach for the shelter of their hotels. Dick felt a sudden, uneasy feeling that things were not well with Lakshmi.

Finally, he got through to Lennox, who reluctantly agreed to meet him at his club, the United Services, in Piccadilly, the following Monday evening.

You enter the United Services up a flight of stone steps and through a dark entrance hall. The porter told Dick that Mr Lennox was in the reading room on the first floor. When Dick entered the dark, high-ceilinged room he saw Lennox sitting in a large leather armchair by the window, reading *The Times*.

They greeted each other coldly. This was the first time they had met since the interview in Delhi four years earlier. Dick had travelled a long, hard road since then. But now the advantage was with him – or so he thought.

Lennox had not changed much. His sandy hair had thinned a little. He still wore a small toothbrush moustache, which he pulled at nervously from time to time. His eyes were still the same watery blue colour. But he had developed the unpleasant habit of clearing his throat each time he spoke, as if to emphasise the importance of what he was saying. This was new. But his way of dressing had not changed much; still the dark pinstriped suit and the white shirt with red stripes worn with a club tie. He was the very picture of a respectable, self-important, boring, business executive.

'So, hm, what exactly did you wish to see me about? I'm afraid, hm, I can't give you more than half an hour, hm; I have, hm, an important dinner to attend.'

'It won't take long. I wonder if you've heard from your friends the Visvanathans recently?'

Lennox gave him a venomous look and plucked at his moustache.

'You never give up, do you? I advised you, hm, four years ago to leave it alone. You didn't, hm, take my advice and you lost your job. Isn't that enough?'

'Oh, more than enough. In fact it was too much. But you haven't answered my question. Have you heard from your dear friends?'

'As a matter of fact, hm, I did have a call from them a day or two ago. They, hm, mentioned, hm, that they had met you in Madras . . .'

'And did they also mention that they tried to kill me?'

'Hm, I hardly think they would do anything like that.'

'Oh no? Not even if I had proof of their involvement in a major financial scandal?'

'Hm. I don't know what you're, hm, referring to. What, hm, financial scandal?'

'OK, let me spell it out for you. In 1970, before Barbara came out to join you in Madras, you had an affair with Molly Verghese, as she then was. She became pregnant with your child. You somehow persuaded her to go to the UK for a year and have the baby. You also seem to have been able to persuade Sir Percy Hancock to agree to the leave. Since then you have been paying for the education of the child, pretending his parents were dead. You have also been blackmailed by the Visvanathans, who would have revealed what they knew unless you kept your mouth shut about all their dishonest schemes. You knew your career and your marriage would have been finished if they had told what they knew. You knew how strong the prejudice was against mixed relationships. You would have done anything to keep it quiet. In fact you *did* do many things, including getting rid of me, Ned Outram, Nagarajan ... and goodness knows how many others. You couldn't risk my finding out any more about the Hosur factory construction deal because that was a really big one. I don't know whether you took any of the cash yourself, but the Visvanathans certainly did well out of it. And you knew all about it but you kept quiet. Anything to protect your precious reputation.'

Lennox's pale face had now gone almost grey. He pulled incessantly at his moustache. He cleared his throat again.

'Now look here, hm, I can't have you accusing me of this kind of thing, hm, I'll, hm, take you to court.'

'Before you do that, I suggest you take a look at this,' said Dick quietly, and handed him a large brown envelope. 'You don't have to look at it now. Take your time. You'll find it makes very interesting reading. I wouldn't leave it around for Barbara to find though. I have the originals of all these documents. I think you'll find that there is enough there to put you in jail for a nice long time. What's more, it would ruin your marriage and respectable reputation.'

'I am, hm, well aware of the contents of your, hm, envelope. But I advise you, hm, for your own safety, hm, to destroy the originals and, hm, forget about the whole thing. It's, hm, past history.'

'Your friends have already tried to kill me – twice. I'm not frightened by your threats. And, as you will know from your friends, if anything happens to me, a set of these documents will go straight to the chairman of the board. I've also arranged for a set to go to Barbara. And another set to the *Daily Mail*. So think twice before you threaten me, you miserable bastard.'

'So, hm, what do you, hm, propose to do now?' Lennox was now sweating heavily.

'It's up to you. You've just been offered a knighthood I believe. I want you to refuse it. Then I want you to resign from the company. Finally, I want you to pay one hundred thousand pounds each to Nagarajan and Ned Outram. If you refuse, I shall send out the documents. You decide. I'll call you tomorrow morning in your office. Just say "yes" or "no". Good night. And do enjoy your, hm, dinner.'

Chapter 17   *In God's hands*

Things moved quickly after that.

The same evening, after he had returned to Hove, Dick managed to get through to Lakshmi at last. She told him that her father had died of a heart attack a week earlier. She sounded quite calm but Dick desperately wanted to be with her.

'Lakshmi, I'm so sorry. I feel helpless here. I want to be with you, to help you.'

'It's all right Dick. Please don't worry. My father was already dead inside. It may be better for him like this. Perhaps he is with my mother again. Don't worry about me. I can manage as long as I know you are there . . .'

'Did you get my letter Lakshmi? Will you marry me?'

'Yes, I did Dick. And I do want to marry you. Now my father is dead there is nothing to keep me here. But I'm still worried about your thoughts of revenge. How can you hurt that poor innocent woman? Or the son, John? They have done nothing to you. I want you to give up the idea. I don't think I could marry a man who would do that. Please think about it and tell me what you decide. I couldn't live with a man who did a thing like that.'

'But Lakshmi, I have Lennox where I want him. He's trapped. How can I give up now? He deserves it. And so do the Visvanathans. Can't you understand?'

'Dick, I can understand but I can't agree. I told you before, we should leave judgement to God. People like that

100

are punished by what they become. Leave it at that, and don't make innocent people suffer. I'm sorry Dick – that's my last word. If you go ahead with this, I can't see you again.'

The line was suddenly cut. Dick was not sure whether it was the Indian telecommunications or whether Lakshmi had put down the telephone on him. He repeatedly tried to call again but every time the number rang with the engaged tone.

He went to bed in a confusion of doubt and uncertainty. How could she be so obstinate? Even her own father had been destroyed by these bastards. Couldn't she see that? But she obviously meant what she said. Yet how could he live without her now? He could not imagine a life which did not include her. It was three in the morning before he finally fell into an uneasy sleep. And when he woke, his mind was still confused about what to do.

*   *   *

The next morning he called Lennox.

'The answer's "no". I won't, hm, give in to blackmail.'

'OK. I gave you the choice. You know what the consequences will be. Good bye.'

In the afternoon he called Barbara Lennox and asked if he could visit her briefly the next day. He told her he had a small packet for her which he had forgotten the last time. She told him she would be at home in the afternoon and to come for tea.

*   *   *

Later that evening, he received a call from Ramu.

'Dick, did you get my letter? I have not been hearing from you so I am asking myself is something wrong.'

'No. Nothing wrong Ramu, but I haven't had any letter from you. What's it about? Is everything OK with you?'

'Yes, fine. But I wrote to you about our business deal. Please let me know what you think of my idea as soon as possible. It's too complicated to talk about on the phone but we need to make a decision very soon. This is the right time. Dick, I must ring off now. Please call me when you get my letter. Take care.'

Dick replaced the receiver thoughtfully. So Ramu had been serious about them becoming business partners. He went down to the mail box. There among the junk mail and the bills was Ramu's letter. He took it upstairs, poured himself a glass of wine, and sat down to read it.

Dear Dick,

I want to ask you if you have thought any more about my business proposal? Now that the regulations on foreign investment have been relaxed, there are lots of opportunities for us. I'd really like you to go into partnership with me. I've enclosed all the details. Please have a look at them carefully and let me know as soon as possible. Now is the time – so that we are first in the market before other people get the same idea. If we don't do it now, we'll lose our advantage.

Also, if I have understood properly, you might wish to spend more time in India now perhaps? With a certain young lady? (You know that Madras is the gossip capital of the world, isn't it?) If you are needing 'best man', I am always willing to oblige!

With my good wishes to you as always,
Yours,
Ramu.

*   *   *

The next morning, Dick took the train to London. On the way up he thought back over everything, especially Lakshmi's threat not to marry him if he carried out his plan. Surely she could not be serious? But he remembered how upset she had been the last time. It made him angry to think of the way Nagarajan had become, and of his death. His mind went back to the miserable life Ned was leading in Bath. He thought about the way his own career had been ruined. Why should these criminals – Lennox, Vish and Molly be allowed to go free? It was impossible to let them go. He would have to do what he had decided, even if Lakshmi disapproved.

This time he took a taxi to Barnes. He was surprised when Barbara opened the door to him. She was in tears. Her hair was uncombed and it looked as if she had slept in her clothes.

'Please, come in,' she said in a shaky voice. 'I don't know what's wrong with me, but I can't stop crying. I've been like this since yesterday. I can't seem to concentrate on anything. My head is full of terrible thoughts. I can't sleep. I can't eat – it makes me feel sick even to think of food. My hands keep trembling. I'm terribly sorry about all this. I'm so ashamed to be crying like this. I don't know if I can even make you tea, my hands are shaking so much. It's terrible to feel like this. Every way I turn there is another black thought. I feel trapped in my own life. There is no escape. Do you understand what I'm trying to say? Oh, no. How could you? I must seem like just another one of those hysterical middle-aged women you read about in the newspaper. But this is real. I thought I was walking on solid earth and now I am falling down a deep, black hole. Nothing is solid any more. My life has fallen to pieces. I was living in a dream. Now I'm locked in a nightmare. I'm sorry, I need to sit down.'

He sat her down in the kitchen and made tea for her. He tried to comfort her and to find out what had caused her breakdown. The cup of tea seemed to calm her nerves. She stopped crying and began to talk more coherently.

'I'm sorry to be like this,' she said, 'but I have to talk to someone. I can't keep it all inside me any longer. I feel as if I was going to explode. Please just listen and tell me if you think I'm mad.

'I suppose I've had India on my mind since your last visit. It brought back memories of the time when Keith and I first went out there, all those years ago. I kept remembering scenes from our life in Madras. I have a very good memory, and the looks on people's faces, snatches of conversations at parties started to come back to me. There was something worrying me but I couldn't put my finger on what it was – until last night.

'Keith didn't come home last night. He had an important dinner and decided to stay at his club. He often does that, so I'm used to it. Anyway, there was nothing interesting on the TV so I started to look at our old photograph albums. It was the thoughts of India that started me off I think. So, there I was, looking at all those photographs: parties, receptions, birthdays, picnics at the beach, hill stations, the Taj Mahal ... you know. And still there was this something worrying me; a vague thought at the back of my mind.'

She paused to blow her nose. 'I realised that one of our

albums wasn't there, so I started to look for it. After I'd looked everywhere else, I wondered whether it might be in Keith's study. I don't know what made me think of that – I don't usually go in there when he isn't here. But I went in this time, and sure enough, there it was under a pile of papers on his desk. I couldn't think what he wanted it for. Maybe he had been thinking about the old days too, goodness knows why. But as I took it from the desk, an envelope fell on the floor. The handwriting looked familiar. I picked it up. Inside there was just one photograph. I had never seen it before. Here it is.'

She passed Dick a yellowing black and white photograph. He realised with a shock, that he had seen it before. It was the photograph of Molly and Keith which Ned had sent him. It was obvious that they were in love with each other but, in case there was any doubt, Molly had written on the back *For my darling Keith – our unforgettable day – and night. With all my love, Molly.*

She had also written the date. He silently handed the photograph back to Barbara.

'How stupid I have been,' she moaned, starting to cry again. 'I should have realised there was something strange going on, but, you know, sometimes you just don't notice what is right in front of your eyes. Look at the date. That was a month before I went out to India to join Keith. They were lovers. I can't believe it but they were lovers.' She broke down in tears again.

'Then I began to think of all the other suspicious things that had happened: Molly going to England so suddenly "to look after an old uncle", then John becoming "one of the family" – my god, he certainly was one of the family!

'And I realised why Keith had prevented John from marrying Jane. And somehow, I simply didn't suspect anything. That's the terrible thing. But the worst thing is not that they were lovers. I would have forgiven Keith that – I loved him you know; in fact, I still love him – that's what is breaking me up. No, I would have been able to forgive him, but the worst thing was that they went on fooling me for over twenty years. And I was blind to it all. How could I have been so blind, so stupid? And as I went on thinking, scenes came back to me – looks exchanged, embarrassing silences; it all added up. What is it that makes us so trusting, so easy to deceive? I realised that my life with Keith, the life of secure happiness, had been based on a lie. It wasn't what I thought it was at all.

'And my nerves snapped – and now look at me. I'm over 50, my marriage is in ruins and I have no-one to help me. No-one. I thought of killing myself you know. Last night, I got up and went into the kitchen. I closed the windows and the door and turned on the gas in the oven. But then I realised I couldn't do it. I can't bear to live, but I haven't got the courage to kill myself. What am I going to do? How can I face Keith now? Oh, my god . . .'

Her shoulders shook as she began to cry again. She was clearly in a state of shock. Dick felt powerless to do anything, yet he could not simply walk away and leave her. He looked at this pathetic woman and realised that he could not add to her suffering by giving her the packet he had brought. He remembered his own breakdown and the agony he had suffered.

She needed help, and quickly. He persuaded her to lie down on the sofa in the lounge and called her local doctor.

He explained that she was in shock and needed urgent attention. Two hours later the doctor arrived and gave her a sedative to help her sleep. A nurse arrived shortly afterwards to attend to Barbara. Dick explained briefly what had happened and asked the nurse to call Keith Lennox and to ask him to return home at once. When Dick left the house, Barbara was fast asleep. He could do no more. Keith would now have to face the problem he had created.

Lakshmi had been right; people are punished by what they become. He walked back to Hammersmith deep in thought. What had Lakshmi said? 'God arranges punishment. We should leave it to him.' It seemed that she was right after all. He decided to call her as soon as he got home. Tomorrow he would book a seat on the first plane to Madras. There was a future after all.

He stopped in the middle of Putney Bridge and looked down at the Thames swirling below. Taking out the envelope, he tore it open and dropped the contents, page by page, into the water. They floated gently down and were carried swiftly away on the current. Enough was enough.

Postscript *1997*

Dick is sitting under a raintree in the large garden of his house in a suburb of Bangalore. It is teatime. Lakshmi joins him, carrying their two-year-old daughter Rukmini. Their five-year-old son Arjun, will soon be back from school.

Dick's partnership with Ramu has done very well. They now have offices in Madras, Bangalore, Bombay and Delhi. Their services are in great demand among overseas companies planning to set up in India. Life is good for them.

It has not been so good for some other people. Barbara somehow managed to repair her marriage with Keith but disaster of another kind hit them. In 1994, Trakton collapsed under heavy debts. Keith was arrested in London for misusing company funds. After a long trial, widely reported in the newspapers, he was sentenced to three years in jail. He comes out next year. People who know Barbara and Keith well say that he is now a broken man.

Last year Vish and Molly met with a serious accident. They were driving into town from their beach house when their car ran into a water lorry. Vish is now severely brain-damaged. He cannot talk and spends his days in a darkened room. Molly was luckier. She could walk. But she went through the windscreen of the car. Her face was so badly cut that she has permanent scars. Not even plastic surgeons could help. It seems she never goes anywhere nowadays.

Lakshmi goes back to the house to fetch Arjun. As he sips his tea, Dick thinks again of her wise words – We should leave punishment to God. Dick felt eternally grateful that he had not tried to play God. God was definitely better at it than him.

Glossary

1. **Indian-made foreign liquor**: the Indian term for European alcoholic drinks such as whisky, gin, etc, distilled in India.
2. **Colony**: in India, housing development areas are called 'colonies'.
3. **IAS**: Indian Administrative Service. The highest ranking civil servants in India.
4. **Tamil**: language or person from southern India and Sri Lanka.
5. **auto-rickshaws (or 'autos')**: these are three-wheeled vehicles powered by a two-stroke engine. They are the commonest and cheapest type of 'taxi' in India, usually painted yellow.
6. **chowkidar**: night watchman.
7. **Parsee**: a community originally from Persia settled mainly in the Bombay area. A trading and artistic group.
8. **Bayswater**: a residential area of London just north of Hyde Park.
9. **crores**: a crore is 10 million rupees.
10. **bridegroom's horse**: in traditional northern Indian weddings, the bridegroom rides a white horse to the wedding ceremony.
11. **Janpath**: one of the main streets of central Delhi.
12. **Mughal emperor's mausoleum**: the Mughal emperors built large tombs for themselves. The Taj Mahal was built for an emperor's wife.
13. **Chettiar**: the Chettiars are a trading community from south of Madras. They are famous for their distinctive style of cooking (as well as for their wealth).
14. **Brahmin**: A member of the Hindu priestly caste. Brahmins are considered to be at the top of the caste system.

15 **Keralite**: from Kerala, a state in southern India.
16 **idlis**: small steamed balls of rice, slightly sour in flavour, usually eaten at breakfast in southern India.
17 **masala**: a spicy sauce which accompanies most meals in southern India.
18 **chutney**: a sauce with a mint flavour which accompanies many meals in southern India.
19 **marigold garlands**: strings of orange-coloured flowers which are used in many Hindu ceremonies.
20 **jasmine**: a very sweet-smelling white flower. Many women in South India wear fresh jasmine flowers in their hair each morning.
21 **The British Raj**: the period of British rule in India.
22 **sari**: traditional dress worn by Indian women.
23 **MA**: Master of Arts university degree
24 **dal**: a dish made from lentils or chickpeas, ground into a paste and made into a sort of soup. Usually eaten with chappaties.
25 **chappaties**: small, flat bread made from unleavened flour. A staple food in many parts of India.
26 **knighthood**: an honour given by the King or Queen.
27 **baronet**: the head of a noble family. An aristocrat.
28 **the Guards**: regiments of soldiers with a close relationship with the Queen (or King). Royal regiments.
29 **DSO**: 'Distinguished Service Order' a medal given for bravery in battle.
30 **the Backs**: the lawns and gardens between Cambridge colleges and the river Cam.
31 **high table**: where teachers and professors eat at school or university.
32 **Grace**: the prayer of thanks which is said before meals.
33 **the City**: the City of London. A way of referring to the financial (district) centre of London.
34 **Tipoo Sultan**: ruler of a large part of South India in the 18th Century. He was called 'Tiger Tipoo' because of his

ferocious, warlike nature. He was finally defeated and killed by the British at Srirangapatnam, just outside Mysore. His sons were exiled to London.

35 **hill station**: the British used to escape the terrible heat of the plains during the Indian hot season by going to resorts in higher areas. These were called 'hill stations'. The most famous was Simla, which became the summer capital when Delhi was too hot to live in.

36 **mudra**: a position of the hand used especially in classical Indian dance. Each mudra has a different meaning.

37 **aarti**: a ceremony in a Hindu temple where the priest offers burning camphor. The worshippers touch their hands to the flame, then drink a spoonful of water from the Ganges.

38 **lunghis**: the piece of cloth which men wear wrapped around their waists, instead of trousers, in many parts of India.

39 **'brides' column**: when a family wants to marry a daughter in India, it is common to advertise for a bridegroom in the newspaper.

40 **dowry**: the money and goods which the bride's family has to pay to the groom's family when their daughter marries.

41 **goondas**: members of criminal gangs.

42 **kurta pyjama**: the light cotton trousers and long shirt worn by many men in India.

43 **paan**: a mixture of betelnut, a red nut that acts as a drug when chewed, lime and spices, wrapped in a leaf. Paan is chewed after a meal as a way of digesting food. It produces a red juice, which people spit out all over the place!

44 **Theosophical Society**: the T.S. grounds form a large, well-known park along the estuary of the Adyar river in Madras.

45 **arrack**: a strong alcoholic drink.

46 **choli**: the blouse which Indian women wear under their sari.